TEEN POET

Selected poems: teenage poet of the highways John T. Cullen collected from 13 through 19.

Clocktower Books, San Diego

Teen Poet by John T. Cullen © 2021. All Rights Reserved.

Online: www.teenagepoet.com and www.johntcullen.com (etc).

Previously published as **Postcards to my Soul:** A Hitch-Hiker's Notes Home from Anywhere, Selected Poems by A. T. Nager © 2017 by Clocktower Books. (…by "A Teenager")…. And other titles (contact Clocktower Books for info).

The poems in this collection are the personal intellectual property of Jean-Thomas Cullen, whose rights are registered with U.S. Library of Congress Copyright Office.

Contact: editorial@clocktowerbooks.com.

Clocktower Books
P.O. Box 600973
Grantville Station
San Diego, CA 92160-0973

CONTENTS

15
- 1. SMOKERS ANONYMOUS
- 2. NIGHT OF ST. BLAISE

16
- 3. FLASH! FLASH! (Haiku Chain)
- 4. RAIN (Haiku Chain)
- 5. ALIEN
- 6. JUNGLE OPSIS
- 7. GARLIC EATERS & ASPHODELS
- 8. THE CAR

17
- 9. OVER COFFEE CUPS
- 10. A WINTER DREAM (Somnium Hibernale)
- 11. STARWORLD
- 12. STONE AGE
- 13. GEORGE & HARRY'S
- 14. T I D E S
- 15. QUIET CHIMES (HAIKU)
- 16. SEPTEMBER AFTERNOON
- 17. RAGA NOCTU
- 18. SUN SPOTS (Haiku Chain)

18
- 19. SING FOR ME
- 20. UMBRELLAS/REFLECTIONS
- 21. WHERE HAVE MY DREAMS GONE?
- 22. TIME-SUN-BOAT
- 23. BACK ST. BLUES
- 24. GREEN WORLD
- 25. AMBER/COFFEE
- 26. LONELY
- 27. ENDLESS HIGHWAY
- 28. COLD PASS THROUGH ME
- 29. FISH POOL WISDOM
- 30. EARTH DRIFTING
- 31. ASTRONOMIES

19
- 32. DISEASE LYRIC
- 33. BARBARA BELL: I
- 34. LIVING AT THE YMCA
- 35. OPIUS
- 36. TWELVE O'CLOCK NOON
- 37. PHILOSOPHER KING
- 38. MORNING I SET SAIL
- 39. ONE AFTER PAVESE
- 40. MOLLUSKS
- 41. MUSICS (I-X)

   MUSIC I
   MUSIC II
   MUSIC IIII
   MUSIC V
   MUSIC VII
   MUSIC VIII
   MUSIC IX
   MUSIC X

MUSICS ONE MORE

42. ON THE DYING OF RODRIGO SAAVEDRA
43. CANTO 1968
44. SHARE
45. NEON REED
46. HOTEL DAVENPORT-SPENCERIAN
47. AGAINST WAR: FALL MCMLXVIII: SIMFONIA
48. PREPOEM I
49. PREPOEM II
50. PREPOEM III
51. PREPOEM IIII
52. PREPOEM V
53. EXHORTATIO
54. ANARCHY 2
55. SAILOR'S RETURN
56. PART OF ME
57. IMPRESSIONISM
58. EXPRESSIONISM
59. PROFESSOR'S HOME
60. RATTLING (P)AGES
61. INDIAN SUMMER
62. STEEPLE SLNLEEPCH
63. CAN'T GET ENOUGH
64. MY LOVE IS FRIDAY
65. DOG LOVE
66. ANARCHIST DANCES IV
67. SAILBOAT
68. SIMFONIA NO. II: SONG FOR THE SIMPLE AND SELFGOOD
69. MOURNING SONG
70. MEDIEVAL TIME-WATCHER
71. HEDO'S SAX
72. BLACK POEM
73. BROWN POEM
74. CAN WE UNRAVEL?
75. ANARCHY I
76. DID THE SUN HEAR?
77. CELINE RAILROAD
78. RILLE FINALE (MOON CRASH)
79. SCHIZM: FORLORN IN THE YMCA
80. LANDSCAPE, WITH CATS
81. PRECIOUS WORDS
82. UNDER THE IRONWORKS
83. WEST HAVEN II
84. RADIO UBIQUE
85. SOFT RINGS AROUND THE MOON
86. WAITING FOR THE RENAISSANCE
87. I THOUGHT SLEEPING
88. TECHNOCRACY CREATES IDEAL DRESS
89. GALAXY
90. D R I L L
91. PARZIVAL
92. BEAUTIFUL WORDS, MY LOVE
93. SPEAR OF LOVE
94. SUMMER THICK AIR
95. DONUT MAN (Manhattan 3 a.m.)
96. SAMBA
97. BUT I'LL KEEP THE POETRY, THANKS
98. ORPHIC SAX
99. KING HYMN

	100.	INDIANS OF THE EMPIRE
	101.	PROVISIONER
	102.	MY NAME IS
	103.	ANARCHIST DANCES III
	104.	EVENING
	105.	SOME CHICK
	106.	WRITING POEMS/INTROSPECTION
	107.	LARF & BARF
	108.	WHY I CAN'T WRITE PROSE
	109.	ODE TO COMETS
	110.	HYMN TO THE NEW KING
	111.	SEA BED
22		
	112.	THE SCOP/BOP-BOP
	113.	NEVER TOLD YOU
	114.	RAIN, TRAFFIC, OPEN WINDOW
	115.	KING FEVER
	116.	SEA WIND
	117.	(THANATOS) JIMI
	118.	GALAXY
	119.	THOUGHTS OF LEAVING HER
	120.	STAY ANOTHER WEEK
	121.	LOVE: IBID
	122.	CONNECTICUT
	123.	FUN WHILE, FUTILE
	124.	SOLAR MILK
	125.	BEACH/FOREVER
	126.	MIRROR TREE/EARTH
	127.	ZEN
	128.	IMP
	129.	LAUGHING, SHE ATE ME
	130.	MARGINAL & FOOTNOTES
	131.	CONS-EN-VOIE
	132.	BIRD SONG (LAMENT)
23		
	133.	LOST LOVE, BLUE EYES
	134.	BARGAIN
	135.	SUM, ESSE, FUI, FUTURUS
	136.	SENSES, SENSELESS
	137.	HAIKU (FAN)
	138.	CHILD: COLOPHON

15¢ 16¢ 17¢ 18¢ 19¢ 20¢ 21¢ 22¢ 23¢

1. SMOKERS ANONYMOUS

The smoker burns his life away.
He chews his lips & bats his eyes.
and twitches & coughs & trembles.

He is like the madly twirling smoke
that issues from the weed
curling gray and pale
around his icy fingers.

2. NIGHT OF ST. BLAISE

broken-chain haiku

a bell whispers from
far Hesper through banked forests
where light is slanting deep
*

hillside rift drowns the
sun in gloomy leaves; Gasprech
bell whispers: "come…home…"
*

soft Hesper bell sings…
(why do they tear my heart so?)…
"come…come…come…come…"
*

between Hesper and
Gasprech are deep, ancient woods –
who knows their secrets?
*

leaves fall on dark paths
empty of answers – questions
also – in moonlight.
*

here's only wonder:
bells echo poor St. Blaise night:
road is soft with forest leaves:
I don't know my hunger's name.

15¢   20¢

16¢

17¢   19¢

22¢

18¢

21¢   23¢

3. FLASH! FLASH! (Haiku Chain)

Flash! Flash! lightning bright –
Sky is dark, wind wild, water
cold – Crash! now
        thunder - Crash!

Truck suddenly passing my bus
tears through my heart:
Wind through tunnel

Falling water scoops
Empty sounds out of gravel
Long dark in rain

soundless autos glide
past, and metal murmurs in
softly falling rain

Flower, yielding, splits
while water falls as ever
on ancestral stone

Sun is sinking low ---
    night will be cool after
    the fire fades away.

Rain downtown: vast sky
full of electric shivers
that sting cold and wet

Rain downtown: loudly
splattering, hard-clattering
in a world of stone

Only one note I
heard him play after she went
to his room downstairs

low bridge: my comfort
in that rolling ball of earth
and sky: the grasslands

soft breath of sleeping
hay: I run through heaving
seas of flower-filled grass

Rabbit: your tracks are
one with the flight of clouds.

4. RAIN (Haiku Chain)

*

umbrella tilting
in empty rain world swishy
hurry on amber street

*

ah empty rain world!
echoes of my loneliness
wander misty paths

*

blind place of gravel
this rainy day – not seeing,
I wait at the curb

5. ALIEN

Velvet currents, silver bubbles
   in the deep
    below an amber water sky…
!To stand on a pearl dust planet
A million miles below a certain
          bobbing bow…
Alone
Among a billion fleeting shapes,
   Alien,-
    (darting silver daggers
      gaping rusty discs
        hacksaw wings…)
   Here is death a quiet dream
   (barracuda fins
     puffs of red dark
       devil teeth gleaming through)
   the end of nothing.
Alien, I!
among the shards of Eden!

6. JUNGLE OPSIS

      **(cautious tread)
  the jungle is alive with the
     timeless patter of a clear,
        sunless stream

patters-
platter
      on green cistern rocks; empt-
                   empty echoes…

      **(tiptoes, a wary hand)
     hanging garlands of vine block
            vision.)
     **(timid tread)
  chattering animals wild movement silence petrified
    **(fear)
persistent cry of plumed
beady-eyed marvel
      **(hypnotic ignorance, fear, hatred)

I Run Back
   to the Beach
   to the Sunlight
   to the blinding Sand

         (   )
  At my back, echoes
suddenly explode in the
green halls of wonder!

7. GARLIC EATERS & ASPHODELS

In our park stands a statue
of the Reverend Mill K. Toast
stalwart founder of our city
in marble rendered to the ages.
No matter that the folds of
his toga run yellow
with tobacco and rust,

And those Augustan curls are
decked with snowflakes
dropped by pilgrims,
no matter.
It does not matter that
those sandaled feet of marble
 tread the iron green
 of a public latrine;
no matter that!
Look into those startled
unpupiled eyes, and
see the future, and Elyseum,
And the walls, like a snowy cloak,
of Athens in the sunlight fair:
There, in heavenly Greece, ages ago,
Lived the god-men of the past,
who intermittently —
...Ran footraces with wands, and winged sandals, and
                        graceful gestures;
...Wielded swords, in their headgear of plumes,
            with vague, suffusing smiles...
...Held scepters, smiling benignly, and made languid
        gestures to plump nymphs all tangled and nude...
But Praxiteles' parlor stank of garlic,......................
............................(fragment/lost)....................

8. THE CAR

It sits on powerful black haunches
A brooding animal in the night
heavy, broad and full of bluster
under a waxy, sullen moon.

Symphony of old grease & vacuumed records.

It stands frozen
one wheel on the sidewalk
bloody, grinning, bandaged face upraised
waiting with shattered but undiminished eyes

for the master
up in the tems.

Its body is battered
its windows are shattered
but it's the proudest battle-
wagon on many a block.

[This one was dropped without notice from my high school literary magazine before publication—tribute to its power, I bet; and I was allegedly the lit mag editor.]

15¶   16¶   20¶

17¶   19¶

18¶   22¶

21¶   23¶

9. OVER COFFEE CUPS

       lowest regions
       highest peaks
  To the lowest regions travel I
  I descend, climbing inward
until I reach the innermost and
       it is the
          outermost
            of
triskaidekaphobia clashing in kaleidoscope with
           triskaidekamania
in reds like the wine I inhaled when I sat in
the gray light by the candy man

       Under the vaulted window Gothic in its
inception whirling with colors to shake my knees
and make me dizzy
       Falling until I land on a featherbed and
bounce a thousand glowing colors like the fragments
of a mile, all in the instant of a space

       the black cloud
          coaldust it settles and turns my skin
into grit, my skin into ashes, my flesh to
sand, like a sack of grain inside a whirling,
grinding sound-mill

       A mile of groans, an inch of trumpets
       they're equal

       I looked into my right ear and saw
       the inside of my face

           a plaster mask with stage curtains
           blowing with eyelashes and teeth
with ladders reaching to a
       corner
filled with despair, loneliness, hunger,
love, hate, want, strain, indigestion,
malnutrition, etc etc etc faith

       I saw many faces with ragged edges
       battering eyelashes
       teeth like flashing lights

       the backs of many heads

        have no front
        like me

        my ears were shells joined by
a sunny breezeway in San Juan Stanicrano
        a lead pipe my head was
shielded in back by a
brass disk
resonant with words
eyes saw me
as the back of a head
that has no front

I fell, fell, fell.

tensions like good & bad
                right & wrong
disintegrated

the stars of the universe
were rapidly flicker-
ing out as I
fell

at the
bottom
of the abyss
was this tiny
weak flame – M E
and I pulled
out and up be-
cause i was too scared
to go down any farther
because I might cease to be.

<u>Coffee! I want coffee!</u>

        Tepid water like candy flavored lead
rose to smell my nose

<u>Coffee!</u> I'm empty. <u>Give me coffee!</u>

10. A WINTER DREAM (Somnium Hibernale)

(Poems Imagining Ancient Rome)
SECRETLY COMPOSED IN LATIN CLASS & STUDY HALL
SOMNIUM HIBERNALE (1)

coppery fists clench
and unclench
in the shivering water
this winter's day

where defeat has marred
our winter and
unclothed the dreams of
the winter hearth

the iron we long
warmed – the sword –
it lies with the
firewood now
cold
in the slanted snow
the warmth is gone

the warmth when
the bronzen-clad centurion
gripped it and cried his
tooth-shattering laugh
in the vaulted brick hall
where the light came wan
through the high windows
and we boys dreaded the
winter outside,
shivering in our armor
that had once clasped the
mighty chests of
Gallic legionaries
and now hung on our
shoulders with the
weight of the eyes
of mute women

maybe the swords
will be warm again

but maybe not

we are far from home
Caesar will come
the Decurion said

our swords lie in the snow
beaten from our hands
by the wolf-pelted
Germanii who
cut down our Eagle
and threw down our banners

the brick vaults
are down but the storm has
quieted

the Decurion is
twisted in the snow
the Centurion's teeth
are shattered now

Caesar will come
and find Cenabum gutted

now the clouds are
starting to flake thinly

a cold dark midafternoon
where yesterday the
hearth fire blazed and
the stars were veiled
by rippled panes
and
echoes laughed away
warm hours in the
brick hall

we are drowsing in
the warmth of the snow

quick signals
wheeling horses

a thick wind is
drifting down on us
that used to make
our cheeks hsine
now brings
only pale snow

Caesar's eyes know
our plight

the fear we felt
in the brick hall this morning

and
the cold of the
battle line

and
the cries we made
before the snarling wolfpelts

now the legions
are marching past
through the forest
black with night
thick with whirling snow

they are marching past
they will fight for us
at Narbo.

SOMIUM HIBERNALE ET ALIAS (2):
NAUTAE ROMANI REDIENTES A MARI

We have ranged
from the
dusty wharves of Syria
to the
silver ports of Spain
our ships have
churned the
briney deeps;   where
arching over Ocean's great back
roll the ships of
many nations
like seeds over the Alpine crests
now Pompey
steers us home
seventy bronze prows
leaping o'er the swells
like stallions
splashing foam
where, in Misenum,
our sails will furl,
our oars stowed,
the galleys empty
to air and noise
we are of the Sea
but Rome
with her homely streets
is our mother
here
is some childhood's
doorway, mellow
as ever with the sprinkled
sun
the sun
which once warmed
brown feet powdered with
dust in
days
of
hilltop
rivers that might
have flowed backward
for all that mattered
to us
but like the fleeting
birds to the west or to
the augur's window
it drew away
leaving butterflies
and
buzzing wasps, and us —
days warmed by a
wheeled sun which
ever farther drew
our eyes
drew them with it
to the limits of the sea
here today
a smile brings from us
tears of joy
and a strange face
in a window long-beloved
brings deep sadness
but passing
we hear the
cry
of trumpets
the captains call;
the admiral's ensign
snaps under mewing
gulls; Pompey
will sail; the
Marines are boarding the
galleys are crowded
heavy and loud
with preparations
we return to the Sea.

SOMNIUM HIBERNALE ET ALIA (3)
<u>MANLIUS AMONTANIS</u>

a quaestor came
to Parvum today

the quaestor came
and brought a
maniple of infantry

by the leaning garden-gate
they pass;
I watched them quick-step
covered with dust
before the quaestor's chariot

Manlius
people were saying

Manlius who had
eaten our bread
and drunk our milk
but later soft wines
Manlius
murderer

Nausea the Quaestor
from Rome
in the name of the
Senate and the People
of Rome demanded
information converning
the whereabouts of
Manlius the Parvan
accused of murdering
a legate from Armenia
and offered a gold piece

there people were mute
Manlius fled, an
old man said at last
frowning with the weight of
many mountain winters' hoar
upon his head

cavalry passed:
a wing, charging dust
mountain cobbles clattering

the quaestor waved them on
and left for Rome

evening dampened the sun
the sun's colors, the mountains,
      the sky
as the infantry began
its march into the mountains

SOMNIUM HIBERNALE ET ALIA (4)
IMBER ET PLUVIALES

Oh!
See the rain
how it falls

silver threads
graceful long
heaven-spun

hear the tiles:
plic plic pliq

soon we'll see
Marius bent

old man with
his mushrooms

dripping by the
fountain there

when silver
vanishes in blue mist

SOMNIUM HIBERNALE ET ALIA (5)
ROMA EXPERGISCITUR

Oh!
See the Palatine
see the Emperor's house
all veiled in mist
and the palaces
like splashed marble slides
on the mountain side

See the Sun
crown the Capitoline
where Iuppiter descending
speaks to the bridge-maker priest
on the freshly incensed
throne pulling his
wild stallions to
a moment's impatient halt:
Feel the power of his
spreading Cloak!

See the Great Circus
with its brooding metal sands
figures trudging its floor
a wheel flashes lazily
once
twice
three times!
on the lucky turn
in the newly-minted sunlight

Now, Rise!
and touch the great vapor
our great City
breathes in and out

a City now wiping
dew from her eyes
—stretching—
shaking darkness off
and catching in her
many-bright-flowered skirt:
new day.

SOMNIUM HIBERNALE ET ALIA (6)
AESTAS AVERSATUR

Smoke
first thing in the
morning

wood and meat
turning slowly in
giant fires

this is camp
the Roman legion
here we will stay
this winter

when cold will make
the earth bare and hard
the grass like the
hair on an old man's head
the mornings grow colder
rapidly

the air is filled with a thin
mist of acrid
smoke
overhead in
the morning light
a flag braves the cold
drifting slowly on a high pole

biting voices ring
through the air
calling to us like
satyr voices
mocking, brave
centurion voices
men who mingle
wood and smoke
with bronze

all is ordered here but
the plains will receive us
tumbling at our jousts
as the sun turns warm
dries the dew
makes the grass cry out
the ground a green sponge
bringing the first
salty thirst of day
sweat and sun and laughter
and trampled plants

from the steaming kitchens
we draw our meal
by the bug-infested grove

then rest in the
quiet wood
tired on the ground

in the cool shade we perceive the first
cool vapors of summer's passing

darkening among
certain leaves

loneliness
of decimated flowers
like the old officers
of the order of the
goose-feathered wreath
who sit there by the
table they three
thinking of Marullus
who only last autumn
made them four

we see the first
gray mist that
gathers in the
deepest groves
the deepest hollows
the most hidden and
encaverned forest-streams
where in summer the
sun's liquid is
best stored and
in autumn
strangely
first paled

gone is the morning
the morning's
exuberant joy
the laughter the
lack of care
our spirit is shadowed

we while through
warm afternoon
slower
and receive cold evening
with a sigh
a cough to the cold
from caverns of the soul

SOMNIUM HIBERNALE ET ALIAE (7)
BRITANNA LITORA NAVIGANTES

hidden by sleep
the Druid shores
gray isle
jutting outpost of a
female yet colder
Somnus
(lies she not
couched
in those long mountains
overgrown with age
heavy with a thousand
winters' dead leaves
as are not the
sands of Egypt
the mountains of Greece
the roads of Rome?)

how they reach out
those knuckled hands
those clawed fingers
to grasp this
rocking wooden shell
how they beckon
those pale hands
that would rend us
instantly if ever
we drew nearer
silence
we have walked the
docks of Rome by night
with their hidden
water noises

—Here,
there is only the
gurgling and splashing
the rocking of this
tiny wooden boat
jouncing quicly past

Look! the far,
many-watered horizon!

we pass now
we will draw close
to the outer tip
of that long gray arm
in a final crisis
but pass
as our captain says
he has passed many times

first
this fast running and jouncing
then
a spray as we
pass the outermost reef
then
the jouncing
without the running
on the open sea

SOMNIUM HIBERNALE ET ALIAE (8)
NEMO PAR CAPRINEUM

The pleasure groves of
the world cannot
equal Caprineum

where we dwell
by cloudy cumulations
vast high growths
of cloud hiding us
from the gods and Fates

the shimmering blue
ocean sphincter
center of our motions
undulating in its
many glittering
rhythms of light
and sound:

whispering amorphs
of water and sunshine
no word breaks the stillness here
which the swans perceive
as they dip down
over the curving shoulders
of Caprineum
sleeping by the sea

and what cry
do the pidgeons raise
in their cliff-cotes
over their
empty-shelled spawn?
mixed with the
hawkers the vendors
the buyers the
walkers are the
sitting, aged, stiff

like an emperor's arch
a tribute,
dances the shimmering
blue belt of the sea
rises in noonday heat
like a belt's fiery buckle
falls again at night
into the liquid cold sea
...is borne rapid and blind
on the currents running constantly
along the coasts
that ever heave and
move about the
hidden sea by night

our limbs are
restless and hot
they move
stroking and grasping

our breath is steam
our eyelids are gone
we move together
in and out
feeling, grasping
restless, seeking,
darkness hides us
on the sand
where the tides lap
back and forth
and play
and come and go
and come and go

gray cold morning
filled with waves and
wind and storm's hints
and anxious hearts

Caprineum
overhung with
clouds like once Pompeii

what thunder
crumbles the
silence on your shores?

splits the stacked
barreled wines
on your wharves?

tugs at the
bright curtains

puts out the flickering tallow

makes the merchants murmur
and toss incense?

scatters the birds
dashes the shredded bits of
their hollow eggs
along the deadly rocks?

SOMNIUM HIBERNALE ET ALIAE (9 ult.)
PROELIA ET CRUOR

the ramparts	
stand in a red sun	
we saw on the horizon	smoke
yellow, as children	billows thickly as
the red sun bears	a wooden mouth
down entrails, compression,	opens
like the sweltering fire	and comets of
of Vulcan's smithy	glowing spit
men move like spiders	(moth-flutter fire)
in their dark girders	follow their imprint
silhouettes	backwards through
echoes	arcing sky
of yesterday's sunny peace	a thousand thousand voices
shadows	resound with hoarse bellowing
today mid this carnage	this red-washed day
there— another	day of Mars
cohort moves	circling raven
in sudden	spins high
array, machine-like,	catching fully
glistening, lustrous	on his black belly
back of a	armor
button-eyed	a glow of
insect with many	ironworks swelterwomb
poison-tipped spidery legs	bloody motherfather
spider	of this gruseome carrion haunt
spinning this vast	swinging booms nudge cranes
web of clashing	clattering with
houses of machinery	chains and crashing plate
clattering gears - -	sparks
tiny,	touch blades hard hard
yet each distinct in its	hard --each angry flash
death	hard and hard: The gods show us
for an eye-glimpse~	hard, hard war.

11. STARWORLD

1. THE PEOPLE

Limbs moving slowly
they came to me
the whispers
the people of the starworld

2. THE LAND

The land
where I woke
The starworld

3. THEIR FIRES

The black plain
of their silent fires
in jars-
stars

4. THEIR SHOES

Shoes
for walking in dust
Dust shoes

5. THEIR THOUGHTS

Their thoughts
save whispers
none

6. THEIR NAMES

Synthe
Vesio
whispers

7. THEIR HALLS

a whisper
a wind
--vastness

8. THEIR LAND

dust
stars

9. THEIR FACES

vague

10. departure

12. STONE AGE

When the rains ended
we sat in the darkness in
our pitiful nest of leaves
and sand in the cave
the bear cave our shelter
during the storm

We knew not which way to turn
which way to flee   We knew not
what to do   what to say
We knew not
the color of heaven
only Earth's damp, dark breast
fertile thigh
wet in the rain, filled
with the crumbling frames of
leaves, and their dust
Quagmire
dust of leaf
dust of tree dust of
squirrel bone dust of
acorn, of soggy, flightless
bird   of grass of human bones

We sat
in our pitiful nest of leaves and sand
in a gray and bathing light
a cold impartial morning wind
tossing a battle-brunted lock of hair, a
playing gloomy leaf shadow
              speechless.

13. GEORGE & HARRY'S

After
comfortable corners
talk at the tables
the pipes the pie
the warmth

They left.

(Light out of a window
frosted by cold
now thawed and
brilliant with sun;
waterglass glorified
with wine by the light:
     a flake of ash
swirling with ruby light,
red in my hands, filled
with the oak of the table,
the window's Gothic green
brown and rust, dark and
light)

Now the clearing-away.

Smell of washrag:
ice smell, wash smell,

steam

Window open
Biting cold
sunlight on sunday

Bleary eyes in blind corners
choked with dust

Waterglass now clumsy and
lacking grace—filled with a
pale fluid in the harsh, icy
light brilliant to the backs
of my eyes

Bits of
sky
drifting, and
of
ash,
and of memory

Ice smell—the
Wine-breath blows away
leaving nothing.

14. TIDES

I.

Ambrous waters gathered
Among the cliffs far out at sea
in a late, red sun,
Like a warm and frothing wine, a dark and swirling wine,
        Clinging and rising into watery hills,
     Clinging, like ruby hills in the glint of a last yellow ray,
           Then sliding, layer by layer, shifting the sunlight,
          running slowly to shore:
First, blossoming out in a queen's ivory comb aglitter with jewels,
    (a froth of white, and fiery drops of oil)

    And then, into the still waters,
        The lighter waters near shore,
the waters thinning slowly on the sand

II.

The sands
    they were strewn like a woman's bleached,
                    cold ribs
Among the sun-bloodied rocks of evening
    and the glazed surface of a green sea
Slid like glass
    To the shore, to the shore, and away
    To the shore, to the shore, and away...
Each motion with the rhythm of a soft bell
              a soft bell
              a glancing bell
              an evening bell
    To the shore, to the shore, and away
    To the shore, to the shore, and away
    To the shore, to the shore,....

III.

The bell it was soft and glancing soft and soft   and soft…
    But there came a murmur from afar
        An uneasy murmur from afar
        A growing murmur—
The sun faded
The wine was gone
The ruby was cold
The fire was ash
        A wind grew that made the waters uneasy
        A wind that made the waters roil cold
        A wind that charged with dark banners and flying spray
            and drove the waters ascending in mountains to
            topple and rush all at once with
            flashing, grinding teeth
  To the shore, to the shore, and down with a crash
  To the shore, to the shore, and down with a crash
  To the shore, to the shore, and a crash

IIII.

There was a
            Boom as the waters came racing over groaning,
                                      battered
                Tracks of stone,
Flying in the darkness in a chorus of thunder
            Through the turns and over the bars with a roar:
Waters wailing,
    Waters singing,
        Waters beating,
            Waters pounding—And then—
    Off the Tracks
    and Head-over-Heels in the wind
    where slower Waters fall back
        disrupted and discoupled, hurtling this way and that,
To grind up over the shore
and burst in a Flash
        on the rocks in the Sand.

15. QUIET CHIMES (HAIKU)

Quiet chimes at night
seamstress sighs, with weary eyes –
sound of cloth tearing

16. SEPTEMBER AFTERNOON

afternoon at Saybrook College

(i)

window

Stone
and Leaves

Open
and Wind

(ii)

Gargoyles:

Strange
where they put Faces

17. RAGA NOCTU

ded. R. Shankar

no no no no no
Twinge!
      twinge of twinge of twinge of sadness
no no no nofills my h e a r t with grief

that this day should have passed and left me in the
moonlight bathing under the harsh light of
the open wound
the moon
      no
      no-no!
      no
      no
cry Twinge of unhappiness Twinge of memory Twinge;
who was it passed into the fertile hills
lost to me
happy but leaving me sad
because there is no respite!
and her laughter no longer cheers my day Oh no
no no no   no no

Melon rind   edge of the moon
Sweet light   white as sugar
grief is sweet because it is full of memories
love   ah she smiles to me from the shadows
where light meets earth
and in fragrant jasmine
disappears

no, no, no grief, no   I am happy now
I saw her face   and she smiled.

18. SUN SPOTS (Haiku Chain)

dappled sunshine hangs
like glowing dew on ceiling —
nor dew, nor time, falls

    *

buzzing little fly
moves like droning plane o'er lakes
of brimming sunlight

    *

dust floats in cups of
warm sunlight: Satisfaction
for the soul to drink

    *

sunspots shimmer on
blue tile, like many windows
    open to the sea

    *

a sudden breeze parts
the curtains,
blowing away
the golden sun spots.

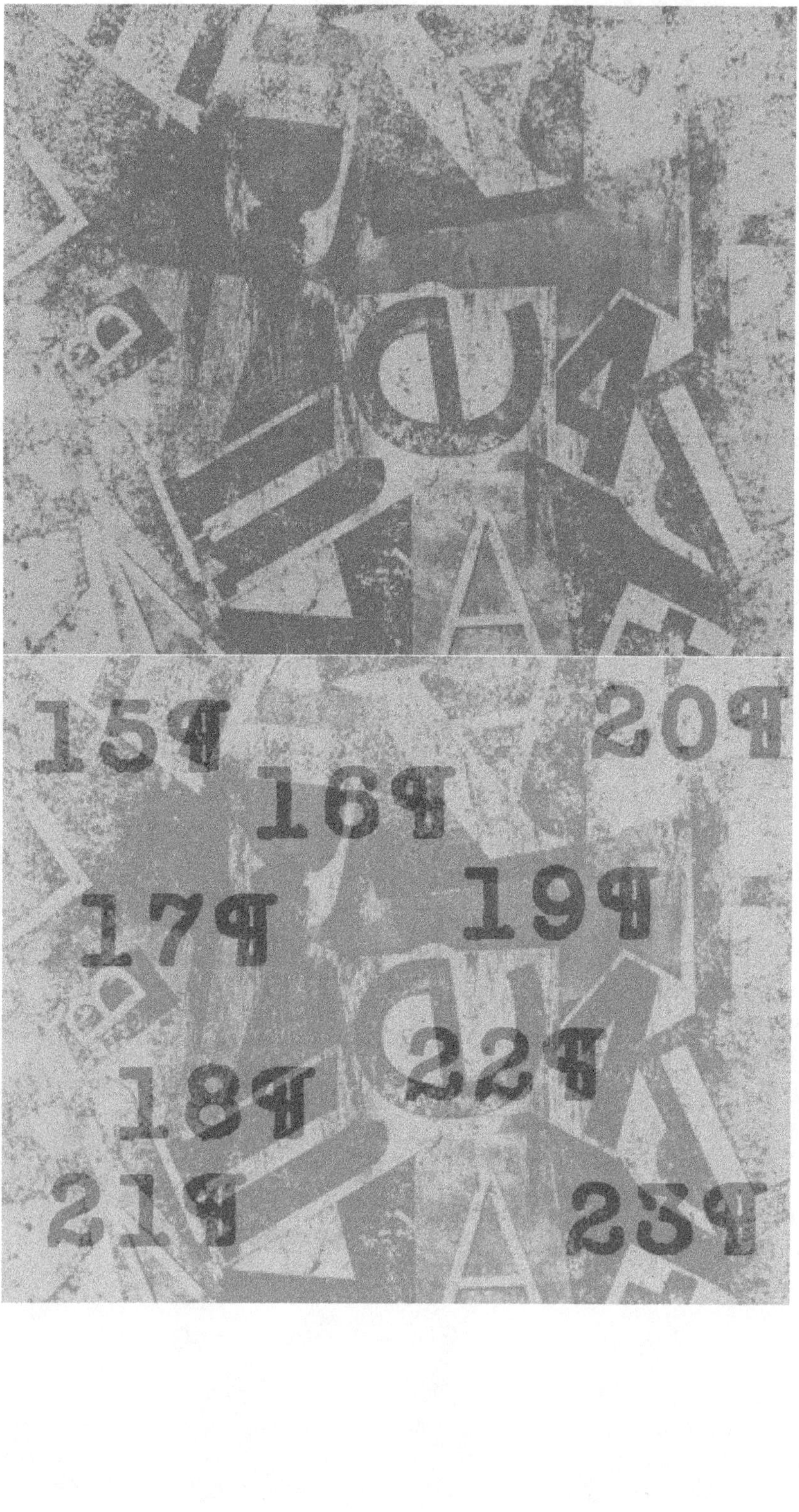
15¶
20¶
16¶
17¶
19¶
22¶
18¶
21¶
23¶

19. SING FOR ME

Sunny
sing for me
a flying-out-
of-caged-birds

by the moss
and ferns
of the
lake

20. UMBRELLAS/REFLECTIONS

umbrellas

in the sunshine

rain drops twinkle

on my toes

when I

look down

I see two people

smiling

in the puddle

21. WHERE HAVE MY DREAMS GONE?

where have my dreams gone?
dreams of time immemorial
to which I was not chained
but swimming in colored glass
I hear the sigh of sound
filling an hourglass
waiting for silence
to tell me it's over
memory comes in a cloud of pain
filling my future empty
with transparent shade pictures
that I know will never be
oh someone tell me it's not so
and you all come around
with your comforting advice
but your dreams aren't even mine
for a while there's a girl
we share the same dreams
but then we cross through each other
and walk along shadow paths, silent
still I keep seeing new mornings
forgetting the night ahead
walls that seem solid
until I walk relentlessly through
give me no promises
to stop the earth turning round
just share my time a while
I'll keep my shoes by the door.

22. TIME-SUN-BOAT

dust river
in my veins

soft powders falling
through lime-colored windows
crystal snowflakes
marching thickly

tangerine glass
brandy-world shimmers
window sill apples sweetly

heart-throb love time
sweet kiss on an orange cloud
heady liquor love-belly
egg skin soft-warm
drops of peach nectar

sky-ceiling, blue window wall
lemon sea spray
bright sails on a milk sea

dust of soft oil drops
(falling featherly over)
over under down and down
softly sleep me in your arms.

23. BACK STREET BLUES

I know a man on Back Street
who keeps a shop for broken dolls
and he loves to make them
of paper mache
and he loves to keep them
when they break

no one ever hears him speak
stays in his shop all week
with his armless dolls
all hanging on the walls
Poor little man he whispers
like he had no voice

but at night I can't sleep
I hear him weep
I hear him in the attic room
waiting for the dream coach
to come and take the brideless groom
to some dollhouse church
where dreams of love come true

24. GREEN WORLD

We sing
in a green world

walking sun-paths
dappled green

  ships of leaf
    drift gently

        where our echoes
       am happy

           we got on

                there is soft.

25. AMBER/COFFEE

good
    I'm happy
here is the amber
of smoke and coffee
warmth and laughter
our thighs are one
we almost
need not say the
things that are
making us laugh

hey

26. LONELY

Sometimes I think
when you can't be
lonely with your friends

it's better to be lonely
by yourself

than to be lonely
among strangers.

27. ENDLESS HIGHWAY

I've got an endless highway
crawling on ahead of me
(and who is crawling?)
sometimes lost in fog
    in picture mists
      filled with dreams
sometimes vanishing
when there are no lights
blows right through you
wind of passing trucks
destination from your
hands/leaves it in the mud
face-down on its message.
    Someone I know
    once told a joke
    but forgot to laugh:
    "If I want to go somewhere
    I'll have to sell my car."
we laughed at him,
but who knows, maybe
they're happier,
    when I crawl they ride
    when I ride they crawl
I've got an endless highway
crawling on ahead of me
I've got an endless highway
pushing from behind
I must keep going
    can't look back
I thought once

I was charting the universe
    setting guidelights
      on the farthest
        seas
I was floating in it all
and getting educated
to expand my mind
to contain it all//but
it contains me
    and I saw where it's at
The past is vast
the present is
a passing moment
the future ain't at all
    I'm stuck somewhere
    bouncing between the
    chewing wheels
    of time's nonsense train
somewhere between the wheels of
present and the future,
the wheels of now
    and a lot of
    empty dreams
    until I sigh
    and lie
    down and die
under the wheels as
present becomes
the future.

28. COLD PASS THROUGH ME

Cold passes through me
my pores
stiffen and hum drily
with Aeolean winds
that shake and shatter me
silently

My thoughts rise
like the bloated winter clouds
snow within
nobody knows
only the snow
in the pit of my stomach

No fire burns here
but the cold unconsuming flame
of a vision of Moses
signifying nothing
in the tangled underbrush
of my mind

Lord the birds
a flutter of distant wings
in the clouds
a million million miles away
inside me

Cold
your body is like the body
of a woman I had
last night
Only the fire of despair…

…cold
I was drunk
a winter's night
or fall
even summer
to me
I was shaking-cold

In the month of New Ember

A crow came to me
sat on my shoulder and
wept
And there was vastness
between my shoulders
old
wind laden with
the dust inside a
wine barrel those breath
of red & warm & forget
has evaporated
to feed the cold
unconsuming fires
of it all

I feel the opiate
opiate of being & being
too dull to know all knowledge
coursing through the ubiquitous
vein-like entrails of
(thoughts)
that hunted, bleeding, gut-spilling
sow

I have crossed the river
not knowing whence I came
Now in my 18th year
I stand wet naked cold alone
on the muddy bank
the coin is in my hand
And not even a boatman
all my cherished aspirations
handful of coins
I think I lost them
long ago

What is this land
I have come to
that it should gloom
with the water vapors
of gray sky
and tell me nothing

now in the night
the mist has gone
the river has become
a vast ocean or eternity
I see now
a city
the dark banks
extend into nothingness on both
sides
the lights of the city
neon foolishness
they twinkle
in the tide heaving slowly at my
feet
the dark banks
extend into nothingness on both
sides
though I think I can see
the tide that heaves twinkling at
my feet
stretched out across the heavens
and in the dark
banks of my mind
wind the cold
blows to me
thoughts
of a perfumed whisper
the comfort
someone passes me
on dark street

amid the banked snow
a pleasant girl

        streets
lines
a straight line is
the shortest
distance
between two points
between
empty
public squares
or just crossroads
I can wander aimlessly
and nothing
will fill the
emptiness inside me
I can stand under
the lights
I can watch cars
I can watch people
I can
I can stand on the curb
and when the streets
and the spaces at their ends
are empty
there I am
there
are the street lights.
.

29. FISH POOL WISDOM

Wisdom
born of
pools of foaming
fish sperm bobbing
on grassy stream surface
in desolate grassland countryside
spit
from the wind
drawn across the sky
(by a boy's moist finger
  in a department store window)
falls
to earth
gray clouds settle in bushes
along a glimmer-cold stream bank
(lazy stream life slow
wallow ponderously nowhere
nowhere just a streak a hiss a
cry of life brief as the flash of a
meteor brief as
a curve in the stream)

gray clouds icy with glitters
in spider-shit clinging
like eroding detergent
in the spread-arm
crucified twigs
dry as bone

a wind
and winter passes
spidershit germinates
busts and crackles
nothing happens
nothing
cosmic abortion
death before life
"Now I lay me down to sleep..."
drifts across the empty road
fireside warmth on a
telephone pole
security —
knows nothing of the
parents' quarrel
the needs, the passions,
the fomenting desires
the seething shrill
anguish of the mouthless mind

echoing dully in the
grating, blood-whispering
bone chambers of the head

the trees
blew their minds long ago
they just are
seek an answer from a tree
beat your head against a wall
nothing
nothing
agony of having intellect
agony of wondering
agony of searching the streets
the long-deserted back roads
the cloud-brush-swept skies
searching for an answer
only a mind could ask
what it cannot answer
mind: a leaf
growing inward
till it bursts
sprays juice
sprays despair
sprays
what lingers
on a night-air tincted
with the faint poisonous
exhalations of plants

(leaves, trees, even
ugly poisonous
   curling plants
living hidden in the
darkness and stench
of hidden-flowing
   swill rivers)
exhalations of stranger
faint toxic whiff
of methane of jet trail
of crashed burned towed car
of comet trail
of star trail
alien and solemn
   forbidding
as the icy Medusa bush
stripped to its
   crackling branches
and gnarly twigs
struggling
half in half out
of the frozen
   winter-night pond
lair of snakes
anguish of the mind
nightmare of
no awakening just
deepening sleep…

30. EARTH DRIFTING

Now the Earth is drifting in the galaxy
clear night Lumen Lumen throbbing
vast vacuum loneliness mingles with sweeping wind
loneliness wind stirs and combs the bone-dry streets
revolve the constellations among stripped trees
Sirius arcs down past a tree limb, twinkles brief on ice
new star's light breaks through
falls a long light-second
brushes imperceptibly a dustmote drifting
                    *

interlogue: Attention Attention planet earth
I am a star
you are a smooth little grain
I am a star
vast and throbbing
my light beams out a message
(look not for your father, I am not he)
message of my presence
beams it one hundred eighty thousand miles farther every second
in every direction
ship without a mast: earth
pulled along, rocking in the wake of
your diminutive sun:
       come you closer   feel my searing heat
       hear my stunning voice   roaring in your atmosphere
       beacons of self-consuming
       destroyer   pounding reef of space
sweeps the wind
    a leaf
chilly water
    clear
glitters a star bending with the waves
    whispers abound
uneasy premonitions of something
    warnings as incomprehensible as the stars
warning   but who knows what?

31. ASTRONOMIES

shark-bite neon
kick me frost-breath
kick my throat
blackfist my eyes

ah I fall and fall
until I smile and say
there can be no more falling

and still I fall

now I saw
my angers
and my mutterings
and the murmurs
of mad moroseness
have no words

:there are no more words:

    only the poetry
      of galaxy-long
        falling!

I closed my eyes
and fell into my mind

died and fell to the shades

pattering beat
of thousand-fingered drum
hoof beat of headless horse
pure frenzy
galloping in Tartarus
tortuous Tartarus

    sable plain
      of
growling hunger
wolf-like stagnation eyes

here I've lived

a thousand years
snarling, white-toothed
among the bloodthorn bushes
of eternal night
in dim and howling
underworld

wringing blood
from a whitening hand
while my other hand
turns blue and cries:

I hear a song
filled with the heart and soul
of a lover
who loves a girl who isn't
sings a song
cries with words that aren't:

c o m e   t o   m e

he cries and lifts his voice
braying bass:

o   t a k e   t h e s e
      c h a i n s   a w a y

but the song goes on
and never stops
because she never stops
she never was

and if I chase this song
I find it isn't really sung
it's just my own voice
in some other hills
shepherding the pieces
of dreams I've left behind
or haven't got to yet

I pass the temples of their gods
the temples of incense burners

empty choir temples
and I cannot say
are they the temples of their gods
or are they temples of incense and
lonely polyphonies?

I don't stop in
so I'll never know
I simply run on
and on and follow distant
twisting smoke signals
taking these notes as I go.

Fool am I
who sleeps the night
in burnt-out churches
not dead
nor do I live
as others say the word.

ah what a smile of love
means to me

because I know
how short its life is

there is no voice
that calls me
by my inner name

I can wear no robe
I can wear no uniform
I can chant no anthem
I cannot pray
only
sometimes
cry (fool)

…Gallops on
the headless horse
When there is nothing
      I grieve
when I might as well laugh.

32. DISEASE LYRIC

I woke up at 10 tonight
been sick a long time
an I haven't seen sun
no, only tired dawn
when I go to bed
at breakfast

It's a strange world I
wake into on this schedule

never know ahead
just what it's gonna be

only
some of the faces I saw before
got there too.

33. BARBARA BELL: I

she rides in sunshine,
Time she conquers, sun time

She's an Egyptian queen
lost in tapestries of green
on a black mare
who's a nightmare
He carries her over fences
stings her with lances
snares her in trances
She takes her chances
because she's an Egyptian queen
like none you've ever seen

She sings songs from a dusky cave
she longs for a man who's brave
who crosses the light-engreen-crusted hills
with sad eyes warning (here my soul lingers)
and points to the earth
far-flung soul's sweet berth

and the hills have hips
   whips and shapely lips
legs wide open to the sea.

34. LIVING AT THE YMCA

I feel
butchered and quartered
living at the Y

everything's neat and clean
clichés and christian virtue

somebody took a toothbrush
and cleaned out the bathroom
so it gleamed
he was queer

someone's crawling
in the woodwork
cleaning away
a million stale particles
of long-ago dreams

but he can't get
to the ceiling
because he's not big enough
and there it's all black

yellow buses come and go
shouting kids, on and off
"our heart's in our purpose!"
"our heart's in our purpose!"
this place makes me sick

I've got the tower window
at the Y
now I can see everything

I see the drops
before they hit
I see cars
in their narrow lanes
before they crash
but only I know when

I see a crowd in the middle
 of the block
where can they be going
all the different people
why do they stand together
hippies and patriots
when they rip each other apart?

someone asks a cop
looks to the law
but he shrugs
cant help you pal
thirty centsll get you there
somebody snickers
and I think he's a rebel

now the crowd again
    looks blankly
      into oncoming traffic
        (waiting? hungry?)

I've lost every hunger
except the hunger to speak
and then I can only
speak of hunger.

35. OPIUS

maybe a stream
will make me dream
show me faces
     and places I
         know unreal,
        but feel,
     and drowns me...

———

satyr

MAYBE
WE DWELL
IN LEAVES

(eh?)

[after starting Pavese's
The Devil In The Hills]

36. TWELVE O'CLOCK NOON

      gray November day
      loudspeaker clears
      his throat and begins
      to sing Christmas carols
      Halleluja, Halleluja
      woman breaks down
      runs down the street
      screaming madly
           doorway faces bloom
           and curl up pale
           in the fading afternoon
street car stops, lets off
imaginary people by a
corner light
      street car runs on
      vanishes on a misty corner
      nothing but an echo
    weeping-wall prophet
    chats his strange song
    in the middlin' darkness
        sitting legless on a doorstep
        singing in a foreign language
        but no one listens to him
  Sing me a song my love
  of worlds crashing madly
  and seas dashing blindly
      Song of a lost world
      bleeding red clouds
      into the grave

37. PHILOSOPHER KING

I am the philosopher king

  I sit on my beach throne
            marbled with Aechaean sunshine

I am alone

my kingdom is within me.

38. MORNING I SET SAIL

To the lost rivers
of a forgotten world
gently my sail
blossomed out purple
on the morning air
carried me
through mossy arches
deeper and deeper
into a clockless day
through a plain of
ripening corn
through a sky
or airy blue
through canal-street
cities   by the windows
of their haunted
houses
glitter-fish flashed
as the rivers crossed
and I rocked faster
on a current madly
rushing   between
mermaid reefs that
waved good-bye
lost among crossing
rivers bubbling
through the
whisper cities
in the shadows
I could see stars
cotton-cloud
sunshine
easing my mind
tremble-fingered I
touched   the sleep-
leaf bank coming to a
gentle stop
weak-kneed I got out
and stood before the
immemorial forest
echoes of trees
touching in the
hollow canyons of
deep
like bright-tone bells
I shook my head
and heard the mellow
notes
of an ivory flute
whispers of a pale
decay
in the sun-drenched
leaves
timeless murmur of a
brook
as I bent down to
drink   I saw
myself sailing softly
into
evening castles
of a deeper world
I turned and watched
my sail crumple   like
a silk kite and in its
place
grew a vast kaleido
scope balloon
now I was back
inside the boat
wheeling madly on
an anchor chain
and I felt the breeze
of passing stars
blackness caught me
up
shook me up and
took me up
in a watermelon sky
full of thousand boats
ballooning softly in a
noisy carnival
of laughing clowns
and
happy faces
friends and lovers
gathered here in a
land of cooky stars
rocket witches silvery
trails
black cats a hundred
barging far below
on a smoking raft of
straw
until I saw
we were in a land
of giants
falling in a golden
trumpet
head-over-heels
in the laughing
corridor of
the great bells
of a voiceless trumpet
landed on a blade of
grass   watched the
flow above
tumbling crystals of
rainbow colors
suddenly I was alone
with empty night
above
sitting in an empty
street
crying softly to myself
I was back to size
stumbling in alley-
ways
looking for the lost
lost worlds of wonder

39. ONE AFTER PAVESE

    We dwell
    in the recesses of the orchards
    mad spirits purpled with trodden grapes

we are
one giant hand
one explosive thought
    one vast bearded face turning
        to glance at the
        tiny figure who is
        trudging up the
narrow hill path
staff among
a million poles
    draped with vines

        (just a glance)
        but he sees
        and hides to
        the side among
        vine leaves

(just a flashing smile)
        full explosion of sky and earth
        the wrath, the heat, the wine
        the phallus, the dance, the flute

        and   sky earth wrath heat
                wine phallus dance flute
    she finds him.

40. MOLLUSKS

Mollusks we trillion
weaned out of
the sand of dreams
    hardened by
    sun
    wind
    storm
    rain
    cold
    fire
we creep to the sea
over a beach of groaning woods
        acid sand
        crystal sand
        red sand
leaving ring
    after ring
a tunnel
growing darker
    to the sea
some stop
    don't start again
        crumble
with every storm
    we dig deeper
caught in the first soft lines
soft water soft bubbles we
push on through a millennium
as afternoon sunlight begins to
falter into darkness' first and
most vague intimacies of gray
    In the first waves we
        lose comprehension
    each wave
        a billion years
        lost, snapped, momentary time
        we grow
        tunneling
        darker
        ah the sea

we who still move on
outposts ever farther separate

                    leave the curling trappers
                    in the cities in the green waters
                    where they wait brightly to
                    share their shells with the
                    lover, the warmer, the killer

no
for us
is only the
whale-like sea
vast womb as we travel
                unravel
                    backward in time
            alone
        into
      the
   darkening seadeeps

I am the fisherman of the
ages waiting lonely and hidden
eons a million million in the
abysmal canyons of a silent black sea
fading slowly
                until I crumble
am dragged deeper still alone
by clouded toneless waters**Bell of dreams

41. MUSICS (I-X)

MUSIC I

takes a
soft jazz the
whirlin dust
motes the
    sun damp
    morning ramp
    liltin tamp a-
hey,
the breeze
flies the curtin
'n cools
    the
    soft
    honeybuzzin's 'n
  sunburst
  where I'm sittin
  in the shade
    just a
    3-piece
    piston chugging on a
    white road a-
hey, it's live
it sings
    Dive
the water's cool
  on
Sunday

MUSIC II
Basket
ball
court
  candy
  wrap
  persweet
  gooey
  carmel
  mel
        up
  hangs
      rolls
            yaybasket!
    now
    got it
    quick
    there
  beat
  slow
  alley
  nar-
  row
  this game

MUSIC IIII

TREES AND ROAD
RUSTLE
car
far
road black and
   curve
near, slow, around
   and
 away...
RUSTLE
TREES AND ROAD

MUSIC V

damp tree
sticks limb
out a-
      round brick
      wall corner
down line
straight and
      tangled crossing
      of many sof
      tand hard curves
tang
le do
wn st
raig
ht

MUSIC VII

papers fall
down idle
to floor
air is
thick
slow,
,down,
,but
soft
soft
soft
softly,
    ly,
        ly,
            ly....

MUSIC VIII

(violent closing hand)
    a cloud covers the
        sunlight as
        evening
            shifts refraction
suddenly dims
      dampens
    deepens
        DARKENS

MUSIC IX

      I
      catch
sight
        of
the
        runner
small
      and
distant

running on the
road a mile
away
                bobbing
      his
            head
      and
           arms
STOP tree
   runner
speeding car   windshield
                  FLASH
              merger
             (?)motion stopped.

MUSIC X

SUN CORE
DUST BOTTLE
AFTERNOON
WINDOW SILL
SHADE EYES

!kick the piano
drink the blues
let im ave it!

MUSICS ONE MORE

But Music, too, Would be a distraction.
Baby   I love and hate you.
your   Voice shatters
music   too would be a distraction.
is   your Will satisfied?
the   night bids silence, slut.
thundering   rage grows in clouds.
whine.   on and I'll strangle you.
Without you, But music, too, would be a
    /Solitude.   Distraction.

42. ON THE DYING OF RODRIGO SAAVEDRA

I.

Old teacher
how time runs from you!
    I see
    an old man
    through the door pane
your sleep is waxen
massive wrinkled head
    laid against the
head rest of your chair
like a mud slide in
frozen gravity-stress
against a mountain
of oblivion
    I sit across from you
    watching as you waken
you are dying
but no one told you
    for two years
    you taught me
    mathematics
    and I
    disliked your class
how I treated you
I'm not ashamed
I feel small
that's more permanent
and
in many ways
better
    we shake hands

you smile
remembering me
because
you were always
so far above
our teenage peonage
great old caudillo
and you never
refused us your friendship
    I've got a long
    long way to go
tonight I saw a
dead car on the
highway, Rodrigo,
charred and on its
head, dead.
    the fire engine
    was there
    and the fire
    was out and
    the bodies
        gone
you sit
in the corner there,
darkness of a quiet
afternoon (I remember
the coziness of that
afternoon, here in this
island of the world's
snows, drifted shipwrecks,
sludgings of the artist's
belly, homeless loneliness)

II.

ah such a sunny January day out
you knew what all that means
and remember, and with elegance
you sketch in the air with
broken words the saying of
Mark Twain about New England weather,
and we smile
        (felt slippers, such as cats
          love to run and drowse against,
"Today baggy blue trousers once
  I   young and smiling in the
am   Cuban sun,
  fine"   white sox (yes, from hospital)
you   over swollen ankles…and
   say   flannel shirt…)
 in broken
 English   but I know you, Rodrigo!
Remember once we passed the cemetery
  on the way to school:
   you smiled and said:
 "…my future apartments"
            you laugh at death
            yet there you sit,
            terminal cancer,
            and childhood
(I swear, total happiness)
        flashes across your face
they have not told you, have they?
yet I feel I am not being cruel:
shrewd old man, tell me,
how long have you known?
When you say, "In the February,
I will be back for teach…"
you forget, child-like,
don't you?

III.

...Tell your story to my friends:
at 11 you left school
working 12 hours a day
at some lousy job in your Cuba...
and you studied at night...
you became one of the richest Cubans:
with trips to Miami, and fields of cane or tobacco,
and in everyone of dozens
of rooms in your villa,
you had airconditioning...
you taught yourself
and they called you,
for lack of understanding,
Professor;   I call you
Philosopher--but you'd
laugh at that too.
When you were in your sixties
Castro took it all away. You
landed in Miami with "ten dollar..
no more!" ...now you have this
home, and are our teacher, and
are dying.
Your wife,
stroke-ugly,
face a grunting
distorted mask,
sits nearby
in the darkish room.
Your two grandsons:
show me their paintings:
they are ARTISTS at 10, 11
and you flash the pride-flash
of paternity.
And what stories you tell,
old Rodrigo,   and oh, how you tell them!
...the patter of rain   becomes the knocking of a
chalk-smoothed   brown-spotted hand
on the falsely sunny (really
evening if you must know) windowsill...
motions, shapes — all with a
word of broken English we
then struggle to decipher,
battering and shaping and
touching the clay

syllables we throw them
back and forth for better
understanding…and full of
pleasure when the finished
vessel gleams between us…
and the struggles of
       gesticulation, also,
are with you an art.
Slow.
Knock on window sill.
muted cadence
in the quiet of your dying
becomes the ballet of
absurdity where it is you
who laughs best, and we
retreat to caution.
"Being ill,"
says old Rodrigo,
"is a question of position…"
clutching his shoulder with
a grimace…"like this:"
(pillow behind shoulder)
"…and like this!"
(other pillow under elbow)
it is a
ballet of
pain
to the cadence
of a muffled knocking
to the shades of
       dark and light
           of the varying hours
   to the arms
of life's great dance master.

43. CANTO 1968

dusk, my lover
soft breast

everything doubles
    deepens
shadows stand
behind everything
and nothing
is without its
dark spirit

the million leaves
are dark blood now
each with its
      black tomorrow
standing behind
and it curls yeah curls
in deeper lines yeah
the breast of my mother
my lover the earth

I hear a tapping
soft blind man's cane
walk, yeah, soft
lapping the tides in
slapping murmur

gives ghost to me
gives ghost to me
lift the head baby
oh off and away far

far far far and off

mmmhh yes
do the gentle pattern
that tells me wine moon
drowning the trees
I have a tail
and gasp a strange song

high up lifts me
to the cream of the tide
softly in phosphor bubbles
drowning slowly in
mucus fluids of elvine
dusk songs, patter of
rising foam beating
the wooden whart
where I crawl out
I get off, baby,
I'm in the toy block
world and I can
count, oh I can count
one two three

but I hear the alligator
tumble sliding into
into, h, h, h, the
river and monkees
scream chatter aaahhh!!!
and I'm not counting anymore

44. SHARE

Darling
I want to share your dreams
come with me
out of all time & place
   to a sort
         of dark
or at least
sort of vague
      world
 of
   soft
        discordant notes

a piano maybe
       of railroad tracks
French antiquity
       smelling of old iron
but mellow with rain

       and forgottenness.

(yeah, we KNOW, don't we?)
a kind of happy nothing

and I'll love you
       and you'll love me
and maybe just maybe
         we'll learn …
              mellow ….

      …passing……………..

45. NEON REED

The patter of cymbals soft at first
wakes a more and more splendid thirst
starry night filled with voices singing fresh
ah my eyes turn inward and mesh
a simple grandeur from heaven spills
makes the night a negative of hills
and sleeping beauty-peace
I feel the longing in me increase
thousand flower girls, tapping softly
urgent tambourines on windborne feet
figures sway gently to a cool beat
a beat like the glistening rain
on many-white-pebbled street or lane
and on rhythm's pearly far-flung line
walks a mellow flute of reed so fine
it spins glowing neon in the dark
messages that make their happy mark
"Love all for the many starry nights

my tongue lies in glue, gossamer kites
then bursts at last to endless neights
"Love all for the many starry nights
and the flute says yes a thousand times
"Yes, love, and seek fields of mountain thymes
cool waters, it's given you to love
endless joy, it's given you to love!

46. HOTEL DAVENPORT-SPENCERIAN

(a flop house where I stayed)

stuffy smoke plaster
here I sit
in the $3 room

world of vomit-blackened
trashbucket
warped wood
strewn floor…

as I sit by the window
in the bloated chair
drowning the
nothing-world in a
few gulps of fresh orange juice

a draft nudges the shredded
end of a plastic shade
out of the ashtray and
against my arm…
looking at the shade
      then across the street
           my eyes streak
           around houses
           over yards, clotheslines
with the forgetful god power
of a good fast car

There,
is the full and sagging
overripened nectarine evening sun
causing cast shadows
like falling cards whispering down
to race toward me,
crushing empty second-had baby carriages
drenching the cat-food&screened porches
the dusty lots, the flags, the rags,
the fallen and corroded fences…

There is a street under my window
where cars battle for inches of corner

and to be first and all those things
(?) whatever…

There is a sidewalk
(let me tell you about this sidewalk)
Here I saw a colored girl move in
      with an old man for a day
Here I saw the owner busy around
      coat and hat tight like cold weather
Here I know a cop is under the window
      I'll be ok if the smoke doesn't
        seep out

Here passes a fractional pie cut of the
world, those in this country I guess,
in this city,
and decide to turn down this street
and walk on this side.

For a while the sun is hidden
behind the house across the street

but across the diagonal
is a twenty-story glass wonder
massive, rigid with its skeleton
of thick metal bones

And there the slanted sunlight shines
lost in the high depths
of an ambiguous flat surface

And there the street is a
silent caveway
filling with liquid orange fire
of some other sun,
some sun that
does not cast shadows, does not vanish,
does not tantalize blinking eyes with
distant warmth

On the street now
men are not meant to walk

only that pantheon of gods who once dwelt among
marble fountains and white columns

and breezeways fluttering with
laughter and sparse, beautiful notes
      flutes   notes

who later hid so capriciously
behind the flowing garment of
reason's presumptuous man-god Father
smiled from behind the grape and corn signs
(and in plaster mother-figures that
          apologetically hold out lilies)
now wilting and fading on the walls
of dying churches

They dwell now
somewhere
at the
end of the
sunshaft.

There, There, is a furnace entrance
where the radiant song-whisper
of a great open car mixes with
brilliance, and, yet, softness, of
that fire echoing, re-echoing on glass…

      and incandescence of spirit
      (yet, softness of human body prostrate)
      that makes the world

    S Y N A P S E

jump twenty-thousand years forward in time
      twenty-thousand years backward in time
      twenty-thousand years forward in time
      twenty-thousand years backward in time

      yes

all in that hot glass, molten sunset glass
but, still, yet, sad, because of that same
      prostrate body
because of a fly buzzing

because ofa street light
because of a voice somewhere
yes, because, because:

the sun
draws slowly
         away.   ******

This place has seen better times;
And I am waiting to see my own.

47. AGAINST WAR: FALL MCMLXVIII: SIMFONIA

(I will never go; how can I?)

        today i am stifled
        sodden and slow
        flower-smothered sunside
        hillsides of wall

        should i be happy
        contented or sadly
        wistful this
        cornet summer day?

        who will sing me
        her vegetable song
        let the black loam
        sift through my hand
        blue ocean sky
        wallowing white cream
        lazy lazy flower lakes
        this rich milk

        i am nothing

        now i am the
        jagged northy hedges
        ready for black fall
        and tread on the lathery
        green hill slopes

        like freshly fallen snow

              today
        drenches me in heathern woodsmoke
        warm of summer ax echoes in bee/bird timber
        timber chamber echoing hot smoke
        hills like the ocean waves

        I am lost in the swells of the good loam
        drowning with worms and ant slaver
        times churning slowly turning worming
        and burning
        comes to rest dashing on the

garden wall
there
an urn
made by a
father of
my father who
went off once
when cold water
was in his eyes
green and primeval
and he fought
somewhere
oh
father of
my father they
are telling me

I should go too
they who hunted in
your woods and rode
smoke-filled horses
coughing helmeted
ghost lancers with
dogs and horns and bright flags

there
an urn
made in the days
of the heaumed hunters
rests tilted away in the
force of the earthen ocean waves
   leans broken and flowerbusted by
      the garden wall and my father's
         father's ashes have been spilt out
           in the trumpets and bright flags
            the good tide brought
            him back to the
   hills

they are telling me
  I should go too
who once hunted here
  iron hooves ripping the earth

  they are carrying their
  dogs their horns and bright flags

                in the rain forests surrounded by
            hell's choking cold black fog and the
            screams of the damned

    no
       soft
    and good is
       death
          here

                i bend
                        and
                    work the
                            earth
                    and juice
                        spreads
                            in my limbs and
                                    climbs to
                            my neck

    god comes running
    down the sleeping
    hillside with
    mossy arc
    flesh hips and
    milk breasts
    and breath of
    wheat-mold sweet

    god
            laughs
            beckoning me
    with fire eyes
            wine eyes
            slit eyes
            cut eyes
            blood eyes
    pulsing rage eyes

    today i swim in the blue sky
    rest on the churning waves

                -love eyes-

she and i
fuck in the
cathedral forests
while the ax
rises and falls
we have forgotten time
   the dead hunters
      choke-stifled musty rustskeleton of
         loam-sunken trumpet ages dead
split, scattered piles and piles of gay flags

:here   in the barking black breakwater
of the green marble ocean petrified
time lost crawling with slowly drowning life

   yea   when the earth shudders
(if you listen closely, granma said)
     stir the bells of sunken cities

drift, in clay-choked Atlantean rooms,
dustmotes and scattered white thought-doves
    over the redwood banquet tables
    piled with white-eyed iron hunters
    ages dead their cough throats
    stuck with dust and bleak worms

     over their gray flags, green iron trumpets

over the miles-wide floors spotted in
places with ghostly darknesses
where the hounds slept when
fair Atlantis sank shuddering
vaporous and cirrocumulus towers
into the tolling earth tomb…

over the vast floors
fly gray doves
circling around pillars cut from a faint green light
and fly ever upty up into the peaks of the
     hollow mountain
    into the shuddering bell that

   booms once
   as the earth moves

                    and Atlantis settles deeper into the sea
                                            in the green

            this is the way of their cities
                                their songs
                                    dogs horses
                                        gay flags
                                coughing foglights

                        is the call of the,
                                message in the,
            cold night when their
                    dirtships belly slide over
            bleak night when their
                    coldships alligator crawl over
            spotlight night when their
                    grimeships stalk over
            flat empty night when their
                    foam ships ponder/cant over
            empty black Omaha night when their
                    bomb ships run over endless torchlit highways
               hack-wing
               swing-wing
            supersonic hot blue dots
                streaking through Cancer

I will stay
granma's lap
still fear the night

sleep

dream:

their whistle ships crash
bloodless dustflies
in the titanic forests of
the atom
   and there grows and grows
            the dusky meadow
   flower lakes
       sunken-tower hills
            trumpet trees and piled urns
                just beginning to moss over and
                    green shapes under them old
                        as verdigris, broken urns, forget…

...dusky waiting for the sun to come back as though nothing
    nothing happened
        nothing
        god told me
      in the tea breeze
        of the
          ax/timber forest of echoing bells**********

48. PREPOEM I

It is not yet
the birth hour
      my soul is ripe
      but my tongue
      is barren
an unplowed field
without trees
in drifting snow
      waiting for sunrise
      I worship the moon
      which shines
      by the grace of
      her fair brother
the act
awaits its moment
      and my universe
      trembles
      holding its breath.

49. PREPOEM II

As I was born
unthinking
and held in my grasp a world,
so now I think
to give birth
      and give of myself
           pieces,
           pieces

50. PREPOEM III

Silent is the music
by which I
played those
earlier songs.
    Stilled are the words
    that flowed in streams
    where I sifted
    bits of gold.
Numb is the heart
that bled in its
great death
    now
        dying only a
        little bit
        each day.

51. PREPOEM IIII

I had the world
and the world
conquered me.

I found the word
the word
ate
me.

52. PREPOEM V

I am drowned
in the life I
sought for myself.

But the Ocean
drags deeper here.

there are waters here
just beginning to boil.

for such was the great upheaval
that it threw me far from my
                          anchor
left me adrift to find my own way
and the way is in my heart now.

(Camus: A letter missing in the
neon sign over the entrance of the
Campus Restaurant)

53. EXHORTATIO

But
no!
let my body fill St. Wenceslas Square
with song and dance and blood

I cast cigarettes and pollution from me
I dance before the thousands
though I'm told that soon the world will end

I can only delight in the sun and
in water glitters signifying brief bursts of life
        amid cosmic death and damnation

                                      Jump!
                                      my
                                    new unpolluted body
                          rippling with muscle and telltale ribs
                          rises fishlike out of the multitude
                          for the flash of an eyelash—
                                  an eyelash flash—
                                  in the friendly sun's

eyes
and my music
makes the semen of an age
once more gush!

54. ANARCHY 2

I am wild again.
Tell that to deanster
               and the provolone.
I'll stop your tanks barebreasted
in Chicago, in St. Petersburg
        and St. Wenceslas
With flowers in my mouth
I will kiss the bullets out of your pockets
and make you blush
when you discover
you are naked
After all the nameless paranoia
I have returned
as always
and you will not deny me.
Bullets will not stop me
when I take back my citadel.

55. SAILOR'S RETURN

      calm has returned
truly, sunset draws near
softly the sea
      washes the brine-white bow
of my slack-rigged ship
      and she lists slightly
turns
      straightens
      draws a wondrous, warm taut
  and begins to run happily along the
  shores of never-ending peace
looking for the coves of cool evening.

56. PART OF ME

part of me is very old
part of me is very young

together
they tear me in half.

57. IMPRESSIONISM

worlds of measured time
imploding slowly from
all directions in ka
leidoscope
colors around all
corners and quietly

disappear in ego-hole

58. EXPRESSIONISM

scream!
make
world-shatter
flight of debris
picture-birds scatter

HOT COLORS!

59. PROFESSOR'S HOME

in this rain-drenched house
the wood walls smile coyly
with child pictures

Midnight reminds me I'm a guest
a son, perhaps, who will be someday

This is a house where children were
and will be.

60. RATTLING (P)AGES

Sometimes I look up
from my droning text

look deep among the trees

idly flip rattling pages back

and bend my head again
merge into passing ages

[Alt title: History Reader]

61. INDIAN SUMMER

the agues of September
are bothering the sky
our sky
    October's burnt-leaf
    (sprung, summered,
    rusted in yellows and reds)
    turns falling
dread the sky
azure sky
uncertain sky
    sky withdrawn
    sky warm yet cold
    sky bright but gray
Ohmylord
we cut this grassy path
    not long ago
this path on a
    shivering hilltop
  under life's changeling sky
    faint ruts
    - - here an Indian of
    our Middle Ages
    might have wondered
        who rides those
    cloud carpets
    swept hundred-mile wings
        manta rays gliding flat
— might have seen the highway
    I see going into the sun
  in my wildest dreams of

    sunwindcities
Martian cities
    (as they should look, anyway)
    Ray Bradbury
- - might have seen that highway
  running into the sweet earth
    upside down
    falling
    from heaven
    into the agar
    loamy miles

while I seek sometimes
    to touch the
bottom of
    this cloud
    but never
    even do.

    H e a v e n-S o n

— dead these
    thousand years
our brother
whom we slew

on this grassy path
on the shivering hilltop
of our changeling skies.

62. STEEPLE SLNLEEPCH

       the steeple
       steeped in winter snow

glazes fogs my glasses
       sings no songs and
sounds no bells
at this hour
of fresh-baked bread
          and newly-fallen snow
in the noon of
the people's winter
       when there is perfume
      on the steps
and coffee flows freely
      in the sodden streets

      the polar day is
        live and here with
      half the night
        but Palomar says
      it's summer on Barnard IV
        and there
          the elves are naked in the freely clouds of
     Augustine's heaven
     and the fresh leaven
of our windy winter
loses itself in   dream snow.

63. CAN'T GET ENOUGH

can't get enough
I'm havin a ball
can't get enough
she tells him
and he tries again
poor catholic virgin
Holy Roman Priestess
can't see enough
in blinding light.
what does it take
to burn out the stars?

what does it take
to turn a marble statue warm?
O marble goddess
let him be your faun
let him hurt himself on you
but forgive him
if he pulls away
when the fire dies.
what does it take
to make flames
in a marble goddess?

64. MY LOVE IS FRIDAY

my love is Friday
she'll always stay
with me on our sailboat
wherever we may float
        I took her from the sea
        in a week of circling sharks
        cannibals on iron-laden barks
        and we are both free
                are we,
                are we,
                she sings to the sea
        are we,
        are we,
        she sings to me

65. DOG LOVE

BY THE fiery light of my last sun
the day wandered somewhere and
whistle as I might
it never came back
only the dog came back
running slow and sleepy down the
      country road.

66. ANARCHIST DANCES IV

Take my hand
and hold it to the sky.

Take my feet
plant them in the earth.

Because
I'm an Earthman
I'm an Earthman

The EARTH is good to me
she gives me hot
she does me wet
she grows me grass
she blows me wind

give me the EARTH
and I'll be good!

67. SAILBOAT

        a powerful blue force
sets me in motion
        all the weight of the heaving
blue-bottle-green marbled oceans
        straining hard goldlight
with smooth warm hands
        in many quick,
            sure motions
all the weight of shifting oceans
gurgles under the clean thighs
        of my white-sailed
        I am
spread-eagled on a deck
        like a soaring gull
          20,000 unfathoms
        high up over the electric
        cold of the black cistern echo-
        waste chasms and chaos plains,
        mammoth caverns and sunken ages,
        of the lunar ocean bed
cotton me, blue sky
rub oily body heat into me
tan me, lull me,
I CAN FLY!
let my starchy white sail
drip and rise nodding happily
straining at the
        leathern bit of bit of fast winds
under
the drift wood
my love comes to me
and we're free

nights are warm here
in the southerly latitudes
the equator is near,
sky of glittering beatitudes
blessed are we
that's what it means to be free

days here
are borne bobbing
out of the toothy china saucers
of volcanic Altantean coffee cups

    we are
    one
    with the
    ship,
    the sky and
    the sea,
    we
    are one, are we,
    my love and me,
    sings my love
    to the open arms
    of the sun
    and the sun
    combs her hair!

I can feel the balmy breezes that stir capriciously around us
Life, we are friends,
whatever time sends…

68. SIMFONIA NO. II: SONG FOR THE SIMPLE AND SELFGOOD

        we
        coughed
it was morning
          uncertainty breeze
what had we done

        bluster the leaves
        sky is fallen and cavernous gray

        stalagmite rain-clouds dagger the earthflesh
we have done the fire and now we are hell

a heavy ringing calls us to patriarchy
but the doors are closed
the wooden palisade is heavy with waxcold iron
basalt rain granite powders

        eyes open
        we are havoc
        see the bloodsucking morning

    I have slain her
the old women call her name
      wailing

our dead virgin

        the augurbirds fire us west
          in the red clouds of
            earthfire

place of amber deserts
glazed with windruts
fire dead
brown ash
brittle,
dry,
<u>ash</u>

your hair is blue
your mouth is a white spiderweb

             your eyes are empty eggsockets

                         on empty road
                    wagon to the black speckbirds
                                wheeling empty circles of
                                lazy enticement
                                to rain
                                dawn

          streakstars
          slide stiffly
          through air circles
          glass galaxies
          fall vanishing
          into the black
          buffeting forest
          of fall's fanciful
          nightmare smokes

                  she rides with me
                         on my jet mare
                    wooden and hollow

CAST HER FROM ME cry the living
CAST HER into your MOUTH your GULLET your ENTRAILS cry
                                                        the
                                                        dead

now she is with me
   dead

but************************sparkling synapse!!!!!!!!!!!!!!!!!!
                         she looks at me
                         we are the living
                         carrying bags of seed

                 seed and floating
                         gardens of arable land
                                shimmerglancing over
                         to rest
                            the earth
                            the dead

           come the nightriders
           living phantoms

screaming and shouting and shooting guns
god save the living
       broken and wandering sons of Cain
egofires
  licking bursting hot wounds until
              dead, dead, dead

yes, we see god, my love and i, we soft slumberkiss.

69. MOURNING SONG

Rise o nations in
mourning-song

She is our fair sister
dead now not so long

Rise o children of Hymen
Hymenaiee, sing

She is our fair sister,
gathered to the river now

Rise ye Vestals
tear the flower crown

She is your fair sister
lost to you

Rise o youth Orpheus
to wind and tempest blind

She is your fair sister
gathered to the boat

Rise, Rise, Run and See
She is lost to us now.

70. MEDIEVAL TIME-WATCHER

    somewhere in a medieval monastery
    a peering eye follows a shadowy finger
    charting lengths and widths
    on a brown map by trembling candle light
journey of generations
through barrel waves
bright on top
dark sides full of stars
fingernail sail with a cross
tattering slow with time
  passing islands
  worlds of wonder on wonder
  lands of blossom thunderclaps
  lands of smoke-fleck steel horses
  lands of pleasant purring kites
  lands of wonder on wonder
candle nears its end
growing large
throwing shadows in the
middle age house
  (dark house
  silent like
  the lips of
  wise men a thousand years
  buried, house of
  torchlight feasts in the
  darkness of
  centuries wallowing
  like huge listing ships
  through boreal night)
leaf shadow trembles
on a marble wall, tomb door
silent with doom thoughts
  peering eye
  grows large with fear
  endless journey
  deeper and deeper
  lost among the
toothrimmed islands
of time's oceans
vision of a
  mysterious highway
  of a future shrouded in night

endless row of lights
(eye fills with sweat)
endless shoaling among the reefs
       land of giant mushrooms
       filled with desert sunlight
       of cathedral windows
       covering the sky
       brimming with
       lost galaxies
       in its multicolor panes
finger draws away
panic knocks the candle out
(eye closed)
complete darkness in the
leaf-demon passages
time's heartbeat
shadow of a copper pendulum
sweeping arboreal halls
(devils haunt the
peaceful monastic tiles)
memory inerasable
gory insect armies
(tears of sweat)…

71. HEDO'S SAX

silver jet
    brushing clouds
      as you rush into the
warm orange vapors of
evening glow

a breath not known
in earlier ages
breathes on your thin foils
    and warms the
      frosty planes of
your pulsing body

whisper:
floating billows
muffle your faraway
   eight-mouthed harmony

    glow:
shadowless on banked clouds
flash   flash
  in the swirl of
warm-colored sunlit gases

move:
    you must not slow
    sunrays will not pillar you up
nor will clouds

keep moving:
mountains below will not

    hold you to the sky

you
    and lone flating gulls

keep moving

the sea, ah, the sea
alone is below
    drawing slowly in
no determinate direction
    with many-phosphored
falling crests and rising falls
    vast and light-sprinkled
like deep night

keep moving
though the sea drawing slowly
draws hard with a song to
lull and blend with
  your many-horned song

move, move
though the sea lure you
into its embrace
with many-hued prismatic
  flashes and dancing specters

move: only   move……

think: Cleo's Mood; Lear Jet song

72. BLACK POEM

into the darkest octaves
my child mind creeps
black on black
white becomes
sulfurous gloomy blue-gray
shuddering with the
blows of underworld
iron clapper in
thud-mouth bell
booming breakwalls bell
fascinating horror
vast Gothic bell tower
in the sky
hollow and rage-shaken
black like rotten tooth
laced with age-blackened
ornature that looks
and smells of decay
intricate and sky-abrasing
ragged and rounded like a
festering thigh stump
wave upon wave of
deepening shadow-shaking
rocks the rat-streets
   cold
how cold it must be
in that hollow tooth
that gaping rot skull
brooding black ice cave
how high
       the lonely birds
             and fly well past

[Harkness Belltower, New Haven]

73. BROWN POEM

avenue of poplars
country road
here linger the thoughts
of a quiet evening
I look at the ruts
and smell vague
pipe-mellow memories
of an army passing long ago
wheels splattering droplets
ofa soft dreary rain
huge horses and
trudging figures in
the wheels of the moment caught
cast muddy and heavy-thought
through many a country lane
always toward the fuzzy bells
of some nightmare battle
there is a photograph
(yes, I hold it up
    into the meager light)
of this country road:
jaunty helmeted figure
smiling at some joke
appropriate to time and place
and soon forgotten
like army and horses and
past crises of
international importance

a moment,
finished as it began
leaving only the
empty road
filled with mud and
puddles, choked with
leaves and vast stretches
of time,
frozen and of the same
mottled softened brown
as the old photograph
one of these days
I just know I'll go too
walk away
walk away once more
but I'll pick a
summer day
    make a photograph
    catch me smiling
    catch the summer
sure there will be battles
but I've learned to laugh
    I'll have my moment too
to me, deathless
the pleasure of a heart-
filled day
to you, finished as it
began
Sepia. Long ago.

74. CAN WE UNRAVEL?

I wish my car was your car,
I wish your car was my car,

******

Can we unravel?
I cannot answer – poetry
There is – too many.
Where in logos?

******

They've tried to pierce Pound,
Olson…Academia…I say it
cannot be done. I am
eyes in my own head.
Today. Here.

Finally, I boil to I.
After the cream.
   --Would be a nutritionist instead
   : Chaucer, Stevens…

But if I pound, or olson,
how? Feed you shreds of paper
for yr bread an w( )?
A find symbiosis…: makes
wine from water?

75. ANARCHY I

The holy stars
tell us nothing

so let us live.
    I must
        stand alone
        and fall alone
        because I am man.
The stars they
tell us nothing
so
    let us laugh
    and drink all the
    sweet nectar
    of our Earth and
    eat fluffy cloud foams
    because
    the air is a sea of gods
    who whisper in
    ancient leaves
    and leaves fall
    eventually.
  structure hardens
  around us
  sea of chaos
  man is born
deep secrets are hidden
and we who look too
deeply drown
before our time
but
let us not mend walls
because walls break

only the wind is free

fills my head
makes me
want to fly

Mend Your Wall,
priest who seeks to
bring the gods down on him
when
they are so all around
in the leaves the trees the air
making caprice of your patchy
altars.
    the gods will scatter your stones
    and bury your bones
    and then there will be only the
    sweet loam the all-drowning,
    the heavenclouds all-crowning.
(So let us not wait
        for the spider to
spin its web)
        (INSIDE:
        THE BLACK GALAXY
        IS CRAWED AND
        BUNCHED SCAR
TISSUE.
COLD AND ENDLESS IS THE
VOID
AND LASTS A GLANCE)
    But let us dream our dreams
    and always dream new
    dreams
    we won't make tomorrow
    come
    we'll be there when it
    happens.

76. DID THE SUN HEAR?

If the eye saw me
It didn't blink.
      near the Nile
         I cast a prayer to the sun.
if the ibis saw me
he didn't miss a wingbeat.
        if the reeds knew it
           they never stopped rustling.

77. CELINE RAILROAD

night time, star shine,
night shine, star time,
night train, star line,
train take me far
to the edge of the city
to my friend at the edge of the city
to my friend at the edge of the moon
        over your iron tacks
through the terminal station
        where we will meet;
past the wedge of the lonely city;
past the wedge of the lonely moon;
across the edge of the night,
across the ledge of the trackless night:

[LOVED THE COVER, COULD NOT GET INTO THE TEXT]

78. RILLE FINALE (MOON CRASH)

Fear
is nameless

it has no name

it has the night
but it has the day

<u>sheer white light</u>

    of terror.   Body telemetry
                                        out of
                                control
                                                    madly

HELP WE
ARE MA
ROONED
AT THE
SIDE O
OF TH
MOO
THI
I
OU
LA
TRA

                    hands to
                    the throat, tongue protruding, eyes
                    bulge like flaming counters tracked with
                    bloody seismograph indicators...
                    ...'irregular.
                    the
                    terror is over
                    whelming in a world where
                    the music is finally   gone......

            telemetry is irregular//radio
            contact is finished/broken
                    the metabolisms of the
                            ravaged vessel,
                            plotting for the gouging hills,
                            have a last, now,
                            last meaningful
DESTRUCT!
                            transmission to
DESTRUCT!
                                    homeworld:
        DESTRU

79. SCHIZM: FORLORN IN THE YMCA

you must have an arm
before you can hold a sword: FAITH

      (1)   a conspiracy of
      crickets, yellow lights, dampness,
      old wood, impending death: bed
      feeds the terror of my night.

      (2) sick my stomach pangs
      the flutesong is redundant
      dog barks hurt
      lonely & all hurt
      Mother catch me to your Shadow
      last smell: lilac-vegetal:
      fading.

80. LANDSCAPE, WITH CATS

On moving in; after night emptiness:
to acquire these old friends:
A tomcat named Joseph; cat-like Judith; and
              cat-Rose with her litter of 5:

      c a t s :   l a n d s c a p e
      s i l e n t   m i n d – f i l l e r s
      i n e m p t y   n i g h t   r o o m s

      ....

--split wood, stacked wood. Built fire-in-place.1 hr
cleaned kitchen:spices:measuringcups;dishes: <u>2 hrs</u>
                                                3 hrs

                                      = home/love

81. PRECIOUS WORDS

      Love is now the only ink
      that sets my pen flowing.
That I should be marooned on such an island,
      Tentacles rippling in-sea,
      cut off from all but this rock.
My thoughts, long buried in the soil
of fiery, unsubstantial imagination,
then disurned and carried in-Sun dry as Roman humus,
in lumbering barrows, whistled-behind, tramped-behind-
              in heavy boots,
breathed-on by warm sausage breath, stale beer,
now their own cave-kept lantern.
      And you, who I thought never to see again,
      Write me this letter of introduction,
      Postmarked for the island, to read me,
      to caress in me the precious words.

82. UNDER THE IRONWORKS

       Here, under the ironworks,
       the calm is deceptive,
       *a deception of forgetful time.

       Unionmen's blood was spilt here
       once when it was summer
       *the iron towers have no reminders.

   nor do they need clothes to protect them from the cold
   because their corrugated brows are not human, need I
                                            remind you.

We are alone, we humans,
with our sadness of eyes---for the ironworks have no eyes;
        they did not see the day
        so they cannot rue the night---
,with our sadness of ears---for the ironworks have no ears;
       what are forlorn evening church bell chimes to them,
       waterlost and resonant in metal gasdrum bellies?---
,with our sadness of smell---for the ironworks have no nose,
      if the weeds surviving oil and rustflakes
       on the squeezed, bulging, balding, cricket-haunted
           grassy earthen rims of circular slag drums
      should give some fragrant flower birth---
, with our sadness of taste---for the ironworks have no mouth;
      and cannot cry against the hungry rust,
       nor can they light a cigaret and stand pensive, shivering,
      hair blown by September wind
      feet still soaking oil gravel heat---
,with our sadness of touch, for the ironworks have no skin,
      Or so it seems, and if they feel the cold,
      lord knows they cannot speak.

There are echoes in the ironworks,
of crickets and churchbells, and faraweigh trucks;
steel ears brushed by the wings of swallows fleeing south;

and a man who gives his days here,
back-bent and sweating in the coke smoke,
the riveting hammering din,

may lose his soul here

in the night:
       see it wrenched into the ribbed towers,

feel it drenched into the gasoline gravel,
taste it drunk with mixed distillation of marigold and
                                            coal dust,

hear it flutter into the blackened oven-chapels
            stunned and assaulted by the clangor of
                      cooling-metal contractions,

smell it fleeting in the ozone of cracked air
                the methane/forgetful plant gases
            the licorice-bakeries of oil and oozed, crusting tar.

The railroad giants
(we once played with, whose toys we are now)
stand silent toward Christmas,
those great button-wheels glinting in little pools of Now
                         on the tracks to Forever
their crackerbox bodies, like toys, still inviting
                    play and pretense…

…though the lights are all out
and the moon is impassive bright

and a black cat hunched on a fence, with two star eyes,
scrapes the moon with her hackles.
                            --I grind out my cigaret.
                          I start walking. I cross the
                  tracks pulling my ankles from the
                  palms of the tie-weeds.
I wonder, though I know it's bunk,
if maybe there isn't a lurking beast,
a stealthy primordial whose skin is iron, whose bones
          are sooty steel jointed with clogged bolts, whose
          face is corrugated with rivets of astounded pain,
          who stands on stone feet
          readying grass claws for me…

but the men are the only ghosts.
They have taken the smoke and the jokes, the labor,
       the laughter, the curses, the songs and the bent backs,
to the tavern where I am headed,
a Bogart, slouched under the revenge of the ironworks.

83. WEST HAVEN II

In West Haven
(west of new haven:

    there,
    was some minor civilization already
    when still
    only oystermen dredged green waters
    tucked away for deep and warmer breeding places,
    called Long Island Sound
    replete with weathered piers
    and small white houses eaten gray on igneous cliffs
    and names like Bradley's Point...

    there,
    was Haven
    where
    alas
    in the 1600's a ghost ship was seen
    foundering in a storm
    and fires were lit on high peaks
    and boats set into the water
    bristling with hands and boat hooks
    but ship and storm alike vanished
    ship seen riding in the sky <u>upside-down</u> over full sail!
    and men and boats returned
    fading into the gray cliffs
    of the New
            Haven.)

84. RADIO UBIQUE

He is the same voice
        on every station
and though I grow weary too soon
and it seems I cannot keep up
    he (kw((24 hrs/7 ds/50w/1000yrs)))
        talks and talks and talks
        on and on and on...

85. SOFT RINGS AROUND THE MOON

soft rings around the moon

these dreams will yield to
deeper mysteries

it will rain

portents tumble through conscience
my grandfather is dead
hence I will die

there are rings around the moon tonight
tomorrow it will rain.

86. WAITING FOR THE RENAISSANCE

I.

Creamy faces: leave the house early
Smooth-cheek boy and girl intentions
hitchhike the meathouse miles
to Chicago
don't mind the rain
the auto people
won't mind you

sincere faces

(clubs, gas, weapons, designed to
crack your bones spill your
cleansheet thoughts dirty your flower
skin I would like to dip
my pen and draw because you
would too if there were   a

butterfly sunshine world
where we could mingle our
warm flesh naked girls
on the brief meadow tossing on
green thrashings   forever)

you and I   we will be buried
and the histories   if this moment does not
             tax the sun
         will remember that a king fell
            and an empire died in the streets.

II.

       Does it not seem
              that these luxuries   too will find an evening?
well   hear my song my music   out of the darkness of the
                              eclipseof this newbut no
                              differentempire echo1789
                              thestreesandhousesare
                              blackfogshadowsfullof
                              lostsurpluspeopleburning
Well I'm waiting for the renaissance the silentintensitiesofa
seems its comin all at once   portentwaxingmoon swept with
                                dead dismantling leaf
                          s t r u c t u r e s
            hunched black cats prowl the
            cobblestones sugaring on the
            howls of blue and green mili
            tia lyingdying of gashes of
            sharpened knitting-needles
We-e-ell it's a night full of moon
and im waitin for the renissance
by a wall wiz a gun, a bottle ana choone
cause it seems its comin all lat twonce

*

He-e-ey this 'us gotta be over soon
  waiting for the renaissance
cause it's a nightta fulla moonla
  I think it's cominalatwonce!
(riff)
We're waitin for the renaissance
we think it's cominalatwonce

We're gonna be soldiers sing!
We're gonna be soldiers
(riff)
we're gonna be soldiers!
we're gonna be soldiers!

we're gonna kill the king
and rape the queen

we're gonna be soldiers!
we're gonna be soldiers!

we're gonna be soldiers
      fightin in the streets
we're gonna be soldiers
      shootin and a-shoutin in the streets

     shootin an
     shootin an   fuckmeanIll
     ...dyin in the   fuckyoutooo
         streets
     like I guess by the signs in the
         sun and the moon and the stars
         it was meant for us to be!!!

the blue line dotted with purpose walks into destiny on the steps of the Capitoleum where the other half of the revolution is guarding the king and his machine guns if I give you a flower will you step in my face brother?

(interlude.   all kindsa jive dug outta every
threehundredyearold nook and corner of suffe
ring because in this revolution baby everyones
                         gonna be there!...fading
into ravel via piano played by a solitary
longfingered skinny mama as only wasps and
teutons can make them……..)
            nearby on the lawn of the deserted campus
            a head buried to the bottom lip in ground:
                        the earth is almost dead now
                        pollution chokes the rivers
                        in the bays burn oceans of oil
                        on leafless slimy tree ruins
                        hang jagged scarecrows
                        it is dark in here
                        and all the prophets have
                        started playing their castle organs
I'm waiting for the renaissance
        I'm waiting for the sun
            a Rimbaud pillar
        a (nameless nameless nameless
                1970 vintage) post
                    carves the initials   of all who died in the
                    fight   they will say
    truly   I'm waiting for the renaissance
        those were the
                    I'm waiting for the sun   lost the dark
        the middle   rages
and it gets rapidly apparent
I can now safely sit on the beach and I know I cannot build
the stained glass windows of the church of my cathedral
peace church of my acid trip church of my carnal knowledge
church of the holy bliss of resting between your legs
while you bite my motherfucker cannot cannot cannot
cannot build them out of random grains of sand.
NOT UNTIL   NOT UNTIL   NOT UNTIL
                the R E N A I S S A N C E !.!.!........

```
                                                            evil
                                                         leaving this
                    III.                               hurt you but  i am
                                                    ther i don't want to
                                                  tell you this mother fa
                                                 reverend i hate to have to
                                              free
                                                 set me free  set me free set me
          Shrouded in bearded incense,  locked in crumbling
          aged vaults  guarded by the fiercest of jokes:sin
          shame of the flesh  terror of the night  lashings
          by the terrible greasy tongs of the impotent state

              adeo ad   adam and eve's precious jewels:   in the
              altare                                     se day
              dei:            alive!  alive!             s!   we
                                      FAITH
              ad deum        god and man are one         drank
              qui                     HOPE               honey
              laetifi        drink the cold water        from
              cat ju                  LOVE               bees
              ventut                                     of th
              em meam                                    e sun

              hidden from us by the insane contradictions of
              mammon's oracles on wall st. which we daily bread
              devour in token of the gods and the freedom we
              once knew  do you understand:  our gods  our
              freedoms  where are they?  hidden from us are

              in the begin                         dies irae
              ning the wor                         dies illae
              dandthe word          cock           solvet sa
              was with god          cunt           eclum in
              and the word                         favilla:
              was god  He                          teste Da
              was in the be                        vid cum S
              ginning with G                       ibylla. Qua
              od  All things                       ntus tremor
              were made by him                     est futurus,
              and without him w                    quando iudex
              as nothing that ha                   est venturus,
              s been made   In h                   cuncta stricte
              im was life and the                  discussurus! tu
              life wasthe light of                 ba mirum spargens
              men   and the light                  sonum, per sepulcr
              shines in the darkness               a reginorum, coget
                      and the darkness grasps  omnes ante thronum.
          Mors stupebit et natura, cum resurget creatura, iudicanti it not there
          responsura. Liber scriptus proteratur, in quo totum conti it aman one
          netur, unde mundus iudicetur. Iudex ergo cum sedebitHOWLsent rom god
          quidquid latet apparebit: nil in ultum remanebit. Quid whose name was
          summisertunc dicturus? Quem patronum rogaturus?Cum vix John This man c
          justus sit securus. Rex tremendae majestatis, qui sal  ame as a witnes
          vandos salvas gratis, salva me, fons pietatis          s to bear witnes
```

IIII.

if you're a poet you'll naturally not
stoop to such shit as this but I'm gonna
lay it on you straight baby the facts of
ecology do not lie these are your oracles
which you set up to destroy the world and
bring you fortune HUBRIS! HUBRIS! you for
got you also have to go   pollution gives
us ten years to live and   we are napalming
nam bombing laos and assassinating every
other nation   So now I call a stop S T O P

        enough of these contradictions
        enough deceptions why should
        the minority who see and su
         ffer live trying to numb
          their agony with the c
          igarets and other he
           roins our king so
           liberally   doles
           out down with
            the king do
            wn with t
             he king
              down
              with
               the
               king

V.
~ V-i. ~

I am in an amber land of drug windows
      floating with kaleidoscope fancies
The days here are full of awesome
      polyphonic masses and
the nights are empty with polyethylene fury
      threatening to gag me with death-rushes

    can this
      ever end?

I am waiting for the candle
in the cathedral at night
when the king's throat is cut
in his sleep
and the queen flees
to the sister kingdom of the moon
and all the nation
drowns in its own red blood

~ V-ii. ~

cut off
    from systematic
    tempting believ
    able insanity,

from all the he
roins provided
to still my rus
hing brain, I

    Bleed

~ V-iii. ~

fear creeps in hot physical rushes
all over the back of my face I
 reel in blackness and the mercy
cannot be soon enough as I fall…
(not soon) fall… (not soon enough)
fall…(too late! I have seen the
face of the wolf
         he is made of white teeth
         trembling tongue slavering
         spit in the cold of these
         siberic forests of paranoic
               prehistory,
  the
nothing
in his eyes makes my heart skip
I am helpless)   fall…
          fall…
              fall….

~ V-iv. ~

   it is good to feel
     <u>nothing</u>

~ V-v. ~

don't say that
  OR WE'RE LOST!

~ **V-vi.** ~

in this land there are no waysigns
we must FEEL our way
by the fingertips
of our
hearts.

~ V-vii. ~

down with the king

~ V-viii. ~

yes. and long live

wheatcheek boy and girl
intentions!

VI.

The domes of Rome fall into the Lavinian dust
and
The domes of Washington steep in a Tarquinian dusk.

When the dome broke like an eggshell
a flurry of birds was born

and where the dome broke
a lake gathered, preserving green
                silence.
Strong Johnny Coatl
of the feathered cap
he put on a coat of feathers
in his pocket he drop
a piece of cheese
he don' need no gun
so he learn to
meditate
an' he walk a
long long time
to meet a woman who
wasn't even
wearin no
clothes.

VII and last:

I'm waiting for the Inca sun
to stick its condors in the sky

I'm waiting for the day
to drown the night

I'm waiting for the messenger
to tell the king

I'm waiting for the candle
under Petrarch's beaded brow

I'm waiting for the airplane
of sweet release

I'm waiting for the king to fall
and the queen to ball

I'm waiting for the coach
to the border at night

I'm waiting for
I'm waiting for
I'm waiting oh!
    the Renaissance
    the Renaissance
....
............THE RENAISSANCE............
....

87. I THOUGHT SLEEPING

I thought
sleeping with you
would be excusable

I thought I saw a woman
behind the paint on your face
your expensive smell & kept coats
and silly hostile giggles
of the lost & isolation ego trip

(yes in bed your body
was very soft & very white
Your cunt made a hot
tugging tube
around my
    sliding penis;
  The soft   warmth of your
thighs pres   sed against my
    legs on   both sides
You moaned and pulled
at me with   your arms)

I saw in your eyes and empty simperings
high walls topped with bars
and the bars meshed with
barbed wire

the only thing the wall stopped
I think was the gray rain sky
the wet scudding clouds (which
bled black on the wall in passing)
because I think
the people they gave up
already and forgot who they
were and what it was that
they were supposed to be   doing
    other than   playing cards
or hanging clothes or sitting
unemployed in the plaza of
the   concrete/iron slum.
      (I CAME---
        a sick feeling---
        and cried for escape.

88. TECHNOCRACY CREATES IDEAL DRESS

loved by men everwhere,
expert says of hospital scrubbery

      women's uniforms.
not bagged in personality,
no opaques to finger for hidden panels,
no checks to make moves and countermoves
no flowerlets to search for hidden keys—
just white, even translucent,
warmed to a shadowy, inviting pink.

prescription access
guaranteed.
Must show I.D.

89. GALAXY

My ship
ridden to   Star 5
reads   Milk Service
the   space suit, overalls
"Milk Service"

night smells machine-like
even a little sour around the gaskets

life is in sealed cartons
lactemus, lactamus hodie…

my name, my destination
my mother

90. D R I L L

<u>D R I L L</u>_____They marched me
                                                                                                        back and
forth
                                                                                                        blip! blip!
blip!
                                                                                                 on my very
own
                                                                                                 personal
IBM card
                                                                                                  though I
grew tired
       and fell
arrestedtried
andchargedwit
htryingtobomb
theshitoutoft
     thrice
hecorporation
s
                    Again they picked me up
                        back and forth
                        blip blip blip
              plus minus plus
              minus plus minus
              Kyrie Kyrie Kyrie
              merging into…
                              …closed eye(lids).

IIIIIIIIIIIIIII NEUTRAL IIIIIIIIIIIIIII
IIIIIIIIIIIIIII NEUTRAL IIIIIIIIIIIIIII
IIIIIIIIIIIIIII NEUTRAL IIIIIIIIIIIIIII

91. PARZIVAL

The words are spoken from our finger tips,
love, you are best to be with,
Helen, marbled Dardan, black Troy;
Shubiluliuma, Hatshepsut;
Antony, Cleopatra; Tristan, Ysolt;
Parzival, Condwiramurs, <u>Condwiramurs</u>!

You are swift in piercing, Love:
My heart seeks you out.

Pictures, portraits, statues,
lutes, pergaments, porcelain;
White stag bleeding on the rocks,
Two lances broken in his side.

92. BEAUTIFUL WORDS, MY LOVE

The words are beautiful, my love,
spoken from our fingertips.
you are so good to be with.

Marble of Greece, red of Carthage,
Shubiluliuma, Hatshepsut,
Antony, Cleopatra,
Romeo, Juliet,
Yellow, Cathay, Indigo, Brasilia
Hymen, Hymen, Hymenaiee

Blue sea
you drown our secret words

Sun, shine, sun shine,
take our hearts to the cliffs

Two lances broken in his side
A thousand deaths in her belly.

93. SPEAR OF LOVE

…You are swift in piercing, Love;
my heart seeks you out…

(fragment)

94. SUMMER THICK AIR

What could go wrong
on a day like this,
when the summer air
is thick and sweet
like a heady wine?

What could go wrong
on a summer day
when the sticky road is squeezed
between massed green leaves
and banks of perfumed dogwoods?

95. DONUT MAN (Manhattan 3 a.m.)

FOR SUSAN JANE WITH?WELL ANYWAY AFFECTION:
LOVE MAKES THE WHIRLED GO ROUND

Difficult without gesture and contortion
but I'll tell you of the donut man:

Dough is the flesh of his forearms;
he kneads, united:

-- Power flies sideways, a hand from nowhere...

Torn, his arms apart
the dough flies up a whirling wheel
bigger than the dimples spinning in the
belly of his teeshirt

lands on a cushion of air, a bread:
spread by separation-hand motions
rippling, settles in a thin flat

Then cupping the appendage
he smacks his palm down, again, again

each time a molested little doughboy
is whelped to the receiving hand,

and tacked by floury thumb –
literally, THUMBTACKED! THUMBTACKT!
to the awaiting cookie sheet.
There to the lit celestial dairy-type oven.
It is the donut — all the world is its hole.

96. SAMBA

#now there is a peace.
earlier my heart ached.
The heart can hurt
like any other organ.
    #Sweet night, I taste
    my imperfections
    in sugar after the coffee
    of anxieties has
    evaporated.
Night time, bright time,
Be my samba, soft south,
of moonlight and
mutual understanding.

Oh, but my heart aches
after you, and I do not know
is it for the mystery of yr song
or the song of yr mystery
or is it really just for you?
Just for me? How so?
I have no tickets for two
to the 3000 mile beach
the empty beach, sunny beach,
where, only in the autumn,
sailors leave for the long storm
in cork boats, and otherwise,
we can walk along together,

strumming roses like guitars,
carrying guitars like roses,
bunched in olive hands
and shone across by two eyes
dark like the hanging mountains
of the moon,
bright blue like the wind
in the hair of the breezes of the
sun!

The pain of my heart
is real, and my hands tremble.
My tongue is dry
and I long to bring you wine.
I will live on and on and on
because somehow the pain always
grows
no matter where I go,
Then I am so lost, so small,
and then the joy of yr song
sings in me again
and I live on
        and on
        and on
        and on
        and on....

97. BUT I'LL KEEP THE POETRY, THANKS

Whose ballplayer would I be,
if I were to sell my tongue
to the nearest trainer? Even
if you promise injections
of Ginsberg, Olson, Pound etc:
fuck you.

I need my bachelor o' farts
to wear for a dressy jacket.
My poetry? fuck you.

Now this the thing ymust
understand: Pound, Olson:
very well and good. But
Pound died at New Directions.
Olson's friends buried him.
I still live, and I don't give a
jack damn to be the hope
of the frustrated, cockpromise of
the castrated, light of the blind,
hypo for yr disease. Find a
shrink on skid row for crisis
as ye pray in church in crisis.
That, if you cannot break yr cycle.

Thesis: Everything
is a hope of rescue
Be not deceived.

98. ORPHIC SAX

If I go back to Europe now

I will carry a saxophone
   in my knapsack
(to play wherever they
    might still be curious)

and I will be glad to return
to these assassination streets
where I am banished to play sax forever
for conspiring to deprive
the government……
                .
                 .
                  .
                   .
                    .
                     .

                ...and the songs I cry
                and the songs I sigh

                Lost in hermetic
                windpackages on [street]..

99. KING HYMN

He is our king and power
He is our golden tower
He is the scourge and honey stick

Semen semenaiee semen o!
O semen semenaiee semen
Semen semenaiee semen o!

His is the tender chocolate prick
Whip and flail to all nations
They/we run to him like his sheep

Semen semenaiee semen o!
O semen semenaiee semen
Semen semenaiee semen o!

Him God gave the might
Him God gave the right
May he keep it high and tight!

Semen semenaiee, 'o semen,
                    'o semen 'o!

100. INDIANS OF THE EMPIRE

In the Temple of Appeasement
are hung some beads and chest
nuts, they hung feathers and
a cracked leather pouch.
As an appeasement.

Next to Cabot's armour
they hung Omitmasin's death mask,
both   are from the ages
both   are dark-cleaming copper
when Omitmasin saw with his eyes
the lights on the sea
when he saw with his eyes
the lights on the sea. His face
is in the Temple of Appeasement
with some dried-pea beads, a pipe,
a tiny foetus, a scrap of
ossified leather...His eyes
are downcast, he is reading
that rindsward bible page,
there is the tally of his fathers,
burnt black under his eyelashes.
The village is ashes,
long sown into the roots,
blown against the trees.
Omitmasin's eyelids are tight shut.
Lights, those Lights are burning on the sea!

101.   PROVISIONER

Oh Heaven-lord oh Lord of Heaven,
it is coffee time, time for cigarets;
there are birds in fading thickets,
crickets, and the phone is dialed in soft
communication-waiting mutters.

Eyes strive to soak in socket-light
but the windows are naked
and the birds tell US, too
of the sun's swift decline in last, falling
              hazes like spring-sprung park water...
- - though satiety eases Evening Lament.

Society, satiety, coffee time,
time of lit pipes, talk of houses to buy,
pretty houses, houses of fire and comfort,
warm homes for long winter evenings
- - places to live hidden
from the glass and napalm Empire.

(phone talk: ...from what mystic Journeys
do men Come To Town?   ...arrive at the post office
carrying bags of Memphis piyamas, Colorado
toothbrushes...have chance encounters with
men mailing last night and early morning's letters,
...drive off in open cars to select houses
in the countryside, leaving that dust and
        observations close to gossip
settling on roads and telephone wires and
shook off on silent receptive tree-tops? -- Goodbye.
Till tomorrow then. Which will surely be.
        and also pass.)

light-song and bird-fall
it is evening in the park, in
the colony of royal coaches,
swans, ponds, swan-pond bridges,
redcoated dragoons, wigged parliaments
KIOSK COMPAH BRASS BANDS, Annheuser-Busch horses,
              horses' bells and foamy bellies...

Oh but really, this Empire was built
of Indian beads, red-and-white face paints,
pumpkins, corn offerings, gifts of fishes,
(gourds DYED brown...DRIED ancient brown like
copper museum armor).

The sports car - - brought by ship from
Angle-Land at the price of Susan's ribbons
and some mechanic's livelihood - -
brings, from the outpost supergeneral store,
the loot and trinkets of triumph
        to this tiny house on Coventry Lake:

- - Java coffee, roast and tinned in
electrically brilliant nocturnal New York;
- - Turkish hashish, opium; tabacos, stamped
tributary with the faces and curved Ottoman
swords of conquered sultans;
- - brandy...liquor...precious, shipped through
the freightyards lavish in tank cars, milked
from the woods, the corns and fruits of
mighty-timbered Canada;
- - perfumes, wine, spicy mustard and
poetries from decadent France;
- - cheese, anchovies, mandolins, from Italy...
also pointed shoes, a caviar;
- - sardines from Norway and Sardinia,
faces, of conquered kings, printed;
- - maple syrup from woody Vert-Mont
of the Mountains Green;
- - leather goods, chewed & tambourined at Marrakesh;
- - oranges, tomatoes, summer suns and
winter snows, from California cornucopia;
also grapes, picked by short, black-haired slaves;
- - alligators, oranges, lemon, limes, from Florida
of the flowers;
- - Mitsui Co. EMPRESS brand mandarin
orange slices from Japan;
also   Zen paintings and poetry; karate;
also
        (for humanizing dark mysterious
            Pacific Ocean expanses:
        SHIPS, CANDLES, RADIOS;
- - cigars and cane sugar from Cuba
    (though we hear there's been an outbreak);
- - coco-nuts and pine-apples from Hawaii,

island kingdom stolen from a gentle queen;
- - guns, beer, lenses, philosophies
from stout Germany;
also, cuckoo clocks from Bavaria's Black Forests;
- - typewriters, watches, from Schweitzer Land,
clearinghouse for treasuries of fallen despots;
- - sauces, spices, peacocks, porcelain,
from our slice of once-Imperial China
- - heroin, toys, candies, from
Her Subdued Majesty's Crown Colony HONG KONG:
- - cocaine, marijuana, peyote, mescalin,
pillicybin, other narcotics, and steel-stringed
guitars from dark, bloody Mexico
of the Aztec ruins
& Mt. Popocatepetl;
- - rice from the Carolinas, brought in
great trucks over thundering roads
to ugly places in New Jersey;
- - salt and Moroni prophets from Utah;
- - wheat and other grains from
the states of the Plains;
- - cotton, alfalfa, from the beaten South;
- - coal worked by slaves in the mines of
Mesopotamian Pennsylvania;
- - Iron from EVERYWHERE
on which mighty Detroit is founded,
and brought on piled barges
over the polluted Great Lakes;
- - cars;
honeyed verse like mead;
powdered boy-singers, swingers, from Angle-land;
also, blue clay for slick magazines
from the rocky Druid hills of Stonehenge;
- - alphabets, algebra, ... from Arabia;
- - from Afrika: SLAVES, gold, ivory, diamonds;
- - drugs, beautiful women, dead & wounded GIs
from Indo-China;
- - priceless trinkets from pharao-tombs,
out of Egypt; also stolen royal mummies
of 27 dynasties or more;
- - BUT
       from the Continental U. S. A.:
       ARMIES AND CARRYING-VESSELS
       ...great armies, and weapons of war
       (atom bombs, atom bombers,
       guns, submarines, etc...) to fight

                throughout the empire:
                …also, vessels
                (trucks, ships, roads, CANS)
                :metal hands to carry home the loot;

I THINK: the booty is edible,
                corrasible, or corroding, and will
                be eaten. Schliemann of 5,000 A. D.
                will find buried in Empire layer:
                "Helmets, guns…and great numbers of
                vessels large and small…"

I THINK: Tho to some the Empire is hateful…
                it would be a much
                healthier, lasting Empire if the
                armies were given over to professionals,
                and if Americans would be
                made citizens instead of field slaves.
                factory slaves, bureaucratic scribe-slaves:
                as it is, there is fighting within:
                "He who holds all,
                holds nothing," repeated Rommel --
                America has no borders--
                alas, no legions to defend them.

I THINK: Pharao does not care.
                HE is interested only in
                Cadillac chariots to race in Texas,
                ships to sail and tennis to play
                in the royal WASP tradition;
                HIS tomb is radiation proof
                and 50,000 artisans embellish it
                with memories of the buffalo hunt.

I THINK: We should recall the Greeks from
                Viet-Ilium with a fast ticket to
                the psycho-ward via wooden horse.

                I think tomorrow will be sunny
                and warm over Coventry Lake.
        That guy will be waterskiing again
                Sue and I will ride the country roads.
                in the MG, top down and with streaming hair.
        The little boys will yell excitedly and
                be happy that they can swim in the Lake,
                float boats, want popsicles, and wear

    funny baggy little shorts;
The little girls will think they are
        little boys
        and do the same.

Oh God, dear God, this evening is sacred to you.
I walk down the road this first-summer's evening
to unload a healthy piss unhassled in the water.
The white houses hang between the trees smoked,
like skins of steers, with fragrant country flowers,
        of hot tar, and fried leaves.
I smile at the Lake, the little Ocean:
        not-dash the waves in thunder,
but slap, slap, slap, frantic for tomorrow,
eager with high-pitched invitations: Oh Lake
who do you think you're trying to kid? I'm one
who has seen the Ocean from two continents; Oh Lake
just be a Lake. Fuck the Empire that tried and failed!

102.   MY NAME IS

Thank you for being so friendly.
It is cold to deal with technicians.
Let me take off my uniform, girl,
and yours, and let us look deep.
I am the continent-conscious,
The lost on highways, the walker by night.
Who are you?   Whose companion are you,
And what do you desire?   My name is
Who are you?

103. ANARCHIST DANCES III

I am sorry.
You have forgotten the Pleasure
so
You must return to the Pain.

As you hang up your houses
and have your cars ripped in half
the EARTH will take your tickets.

104. EVENING

Ten Thousand Fires
autumn sun crowned grassy woodland
   so very long ago

      and where swallows drowned in
                evening's spires
bells sang together in drowsy dusk

not a word was said
    and before long
it was all dark and over.

105. SOME CHICK

tho you want your *big car*
your nice house, Jane,
and tho you leave the revolution,
will you change the world
the way you change yr head?
    I mean, why do we live?
    Is it all to have a house
    so that 50 others must
    stand outside?
    Is it to drive a car
    so that 100 others
    must walk?
and once you become the oppressor,
will the world, too, stop being oppressed?
will the oppressed no longer fight your kind?

and would you build a house
     for waiting?   I mean
     will you work (for <u>what?</u>)
     to a future that simply isn't?
    will you have yr car (driving
    to the supermarket or work
    or any plaguish thing) so
    that on yr salvation day
    you can drive (out of yr house cocoon
    that final highway to
    the great release?
    --do you expect top hats
    tail coats and carnations
    on that day of

      wedding/inauguration
       /others, yr pipe dreams?

106. WRITING POEMS/INTROSPECTION

(Sue)
at 3 a.m.
<u>one thinks the strangest things</u>

in 12 hours I will be
sucked into the sky shot over
a cloud dragged through the hills
<u>dropped in New Haven</u>

I am fearful of this new forest
I don't want to look too deep
for fear of the face, the eyes, looking back

tonight I saw the pond
and looked past the glitters
at the sunken worlds
bittenoff ends of mourning dragwillows

I will not go to your castle
because there am I
and because I fear your dungeons
chain and pounding weary mallets

      bottle of blood
      I have prickled my hand
      on a foreboding thorn

oh forest
if you knew

the things I have seen

the cities I have stood and wept in
the transdimensional highways I have hitched
  run through by fast cars
  and barreling truck monsters

        but forest
          your leaves can only titter
            because you have been so
well hidden
          from the misty corners
                the shrouded
mourners
from the drinkers, the thinkers, the shrinkers
  the rats, the bats, the party hats

forest you are so like a woman
a place to wait, a place too late
a time to stop and explore
(a fool on a horse has also said)

no: you are for the butterflies
branch to branch, flower to flower
and never a rest

  I am not for castles on hilltops
    in deep dark forests
where there is an occasional sunny meadow
but mostly
a gloomy
pain

oh forest
I've looked too deep already
which is why I run back to my
stone mistress the highway
where is no rest

this you cannot understand

there were many cities
there will be many more
 -or do you know of these?
  will you surprise me again?-
with lots inbetween
and nothing there

        should I be a wagon wheel
        half buried in a heady yet
        painful loam sunk to the
        hub not to move again
        subject to caprice?

I will remember you forest
you will flow burning and blue
onto paper at Wall St.'s G&H
wooden hideaway

you will be in my mind in
my hearth in my eyes

I will come in the morning
to sit by the benches we carved on
my friends and I
long ago
I will write my poems
smoke my cigarettes drink my coffee

talk distantly to the alley-eye
people
and wonder
what it could have been like
in the castle on the hilltop in
the dark forest,
and why I didn't go to see.

107.   LARF & BARF

ON...VOLUME...

Pleasant chords from a guitar
drove me to sunshine land
on a wagon without wheels
into a KRISPI cowlike sunset
wiped by a twitching tail
(airs of shimmering nothing-child)
supermarket evening heels
lipstick cigarette and shopping bag

curses
for the hour and the table
curses for the fun and the life
       the Live and (in Sunday's black
       misappropriated book) the Die.

somewhere behind a
   Larf & Barf billboard
hidden by brick walls and
   the trash eking out of suburbia's pores
is the message, the massage, the orgasm:

WEAT TV CHANNEL I, NY

take and eat
this is my trash

MOSTESS BREAD, KEEP YOU FED

take and drink
this is my bile

HEY YOU, SUBURBANITE!
FRED! JOE! SPIKE! HAPPY!
MURIEL! SALLY! DROOLCUNT!

what are you going here in heaven?
look at you. just look at you.
you're a mess, charley brown.

YOU'RE DULL. YOU'RE FAT.

On**
drink this my bile
to the full of your festering brim
your crusted lips
your banana-black cheeks
your calorie-burnt red eyes.

YOU'RE STILL SICKENING!
YOU'RE UNBEAUTIFUL!
YOU DON'T BELONG HERE
IN HEAVEN (Buy this, buy
this, we'll give you another chance)

WHY CAN'T YOU BE LIKE U S????????????!!!!!!!!!!!!!!!

curse   then
the day you made on your clock,
the house you built to pattern,
the clothes you buy to prescription,
the cigarets you smoke to perdition,
the pills you eat for your condition,
the hymns you sing to LARF & BARF
oo, yukkity-yukkity-yurf yurf yurf!
  (slobberndrool!)   (chykyuppp!)

(your hair is cut short so that I can't see you when
you stand in the earth under your lawn)

   YOU   HAVE   BAD   BREATH

you get those head-aches
watching aspiring commercials

   YOU   EAT   SHIT!

(this is the voice of culcha,
brought to you by Kleenex[r])

you get thirsty
watching soda ads
and after you've run & drunk a can
you're puzzled and deflated
when they ignore you
and send you for another
(in a friendly way)

They're out to quench a thirst you never had, asshole.

ON...VERT...HORIZ...
                      and they build a thirst
                      you'll never know you have
CONTRAST...FINE...TUNING...
                      feel the burning in your throat
                      you won't know what you died of
DO NOT ATTEMPT TO REMOVE BACK PANEL – a trained repairman
will do it if you promise not to peek-G O .   L E T   M E
S L E E P . . . .

**Off.

108.   WHY I CAN'T WRITE PROSE

        (I smoked cigarets)...and
        discovered suddenly tonight
        why I cannot write prose.

        It is because Mr. Smith does This
        Mrs. Smith says That;
        Emma wonders if her lipstick smears;
        Sanchez cuts his beard off
        because it rhymes with cleared-off

        and there is no mystery
        in why they all live on.

109.   ODE TO COMETS

G O S - S P E L —goodnews—
spreading!

we are in a blind place
full of atomic lights.

It is dark under the stars
and a Chinese bell
tolls news through the yards.

      Men are gathered
      to watch the sky
      through lenses of tears
      and the bronze telescope
      stands unused, painted
      by Galileo Galilei.

Those who sampled herbs
on the sleepy banks of Assur
gather pensive cloaks here
under this heretic paroply
and News of new discoveries
twinkles over the ocean tides
    from other kingdoms.
    --the stars are tiny holes in the sky
    says a man of Eire;
    --next a turtle holds up the earth
    says the Mohauk sage;
    --also we are discovering that the earth is a
flat disc
brimming with water on which the continents
like milksops float---
(Hush!) the priests of plastic Juice spitter
  have spies everywhere though at night they stay
    locked in the Star-Chambers for fear of
      their own demons.
Yes there are demons all around
though exorcism is done by mail
and no priest has heresied in years.
--we are discovering, drawing catalogs:
  Horus, Isis, Jesus, Manitou, Magna Mater...
--we dare to claim new worlds, draw new cartographies:
  Elysium, Eden, Shangri-la, Castalia, Middle Earth...

            ...once upon a time...   ...here there be
                        painted sea horses   and
                                            friendly Nessies...
        They say Kopernick is multiplying gold from leaden balls in Krakow
     Isabel has choked the madman Columbo on his his unethick lust for gold,
And Tetzel only yesterday   souled a thousand souls   a thousand cures!
                    A sailor from a boreal mountain kingdom
                    has cupped his hands in the waters of a
                    tropic volcano lake and brought forth
                    from the green water   radiant eggs,
                    from a hidden river,   whose mothers
                    were gold sea dragons,   their father
                    the west wind   and brought them back
                    to test for magic words and cryptic incantations,
                    binding spells loosed only by the knot of
                    certain conjunctions of the spheres of the
                    musical universe.
O ye comets that ring this mystery-black universe!
            Coelum coelorum coelorississimorum!
there are ages to set back, earths to dig,
roots to rub with clay-smeared fingers,
seas to cut with   boat knives!
############### 21 ################

110.   HYMN TO THE NEW KING

Come let us sail away,
let's fill our sails with wind
toward the morning sun.

Let the briny deeps of the sea
raise white fingers
to carress my ship's bow.

Sing, ye maidens waiting
on the shore, the glories of
Helen, & of your new-found king.

Our fathers' heavy-bearded
faces stare out from the waves
nodding solemn assent…

111.   SEA BED

My bed is my sea-bed.
There I soak-in-green-dessication,
Soaped by butterflies of sunlight.
The sea can be held in a bath tub,
even in a thimble.

In that faint glimmering of consciousness
Sleep is deep as the wordless womb.
Marble tomb flooded by sea water.
--Sending trillion-kilowatt hoarse whispers
to my neighbor Draco Pulsar, *Om*,
says Draco, --*Shanti*, chirps
the echoing basilica with nuns' voices.
The stones answer in voices of stone.

I am I-less. Probed by the
Panicked but dully glad feelers
of my ego-head. "Awake," it says
in a faint, far voice, "awake!"
You owe it to yourself.

It is the voice that writes
Odes addressing the
sea-hanging cliffs.

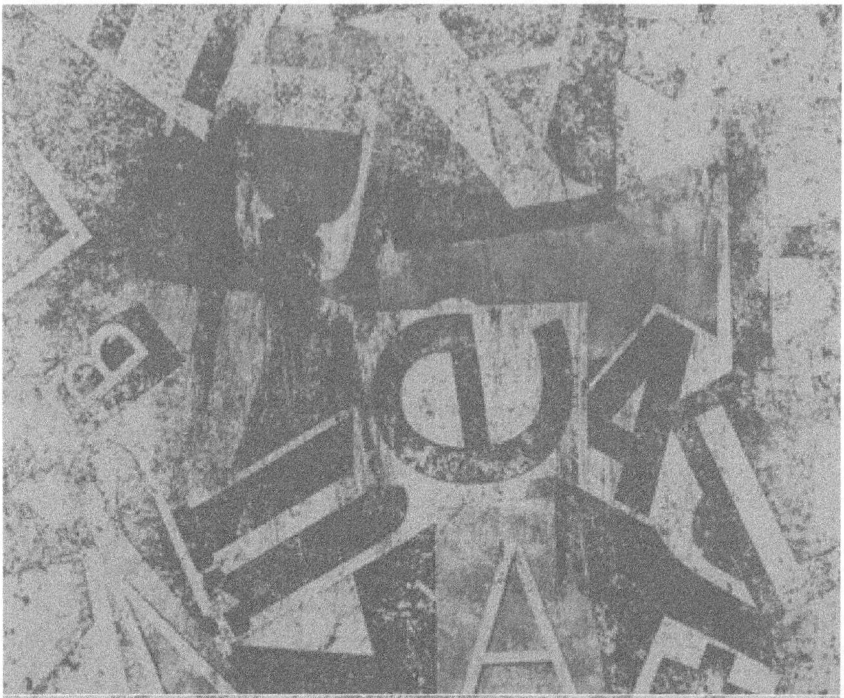

15¶
20¶
16¶
17¶
19¶
22¶
18¶
21¶
23¶

112. THE SCOP/BOP-BOP

    damn the delft Elizabethans
Hokey, beep beep, you suck the cock,
having words in the subway, his
    testament is on the wall,
his testicles are rapt around the rails.
We are holding back Nothing
this morning of our Ever.
Oh fair Eve   I want to fuck you
literally   I want to swyve you,
to stick it in you, make your eyes roll.
cream, cream, cream. We speak in
    shattered syndactyls. This is release.
Broken, the promise is shattered.
It was only words. Do you understand?
We are all Indians.

113. NEVER TOLD YOU

Brown-eyed girl, I love you
and I never said a word.
Behind the shadows of my skin
I hid a sleeping flower bud
and when it would not open
I hid it from myself and
there it remains, reminding me
of you sometimes, of you,
brown-eyed girl.

114. RAIN, TRAFFIC, OPEN WINDOW

afterthoughts, the   aftertaste
bares my champagne
   to the   empty apartment.
rain, traffic, open window.

-and you   on some night curb-
-a prism for your thoughts-
a tear drop, a sip of my   champagne.

115. KING FEVER

The cities are sister-wives of the king.
Harem slaves the conquered foreign ports.
Men are stick figures
sweating over womanly ships.
Everywhere is the king, fucking.

(Renaissance)

116.   SEA WIND

Making peace with my destiny
I go to the islands.
No more winter this heart
I sun like soap.
You my love, with me
Would have it no other way.
A ship, darling, a ship
Waits at dawn, dewy sails.
Waits at dawn mist-hung
Rocking salty by green stones.
A captain and a sailor there
come to cheer falling sails.
A captain and a sailor there
come to cheer rising seas.
Briney gale whistles eerily
 in the nostrils of my skull,
Howls salty Glorias
while the good-bye boy
      madly shakes
      the ship's bell.
Briney wind rubs our eyeballs
The wind, morning muezzin.
Pre-sun, dim pearls the sea-drops
The wind, rubbing our backs.

117.   (THANATOS) JIMI

    Jimi –
    your guitaring stopped
    and the newsmen said
    that you are dead.
I feel very humble
because a gate has been laid
over the cellars of the sea.
    your
    trains clattered in the rain
    your
    blood-voodoo frenzied
    red thoughts
    your
    love was mystic,
    baying in the moon
    your
    voice/guitar was wireless
     from Atlantis
    Your
    beauty was transfixing
        your colors were music:
rainforest, green
firebelly, purple
alabaster, Aegean: white
red – robe of sacrifice/mystery

sky-kissing <u>blue</u>
black of lone watchtowers
    (like Catholic
    mystery colors)
your words:
snow white flour
to the music paste
the manic haste
the electric caste
the downy waist
to the   final waste.
    HENDRIX –
    did the sky fall out from
    under you?
    --leave you with a needle
    in your stiffened vein,
       a glassy madness
    in your bulging eyes –
    marbled & rolling
    in the rather surprising
    orgasm of End?
Still I have yr old records
to listen to
and wonder what the world
really was.

118. GALAXY

I am moved to
swoone and trembling
love with clasped hands
when I think that
this poet has captured
my childhood's oil puddle
(of the day I stood blue
and hurt under the iron bridge,
              intoxicated
with the gritty air smell of
locomotive-burning)
or that poet has
understood how at night, in the mansard,
I listened (arm dangling
restlessly over concrete
and stucco) to cars
on the *Escherstross*
incising my meadows and
my forests with aerospace portents.

119. THOUGHTS OF LEAVING HER

MORNING TWILIGHT ON THE BED   COVERLESS BESIDE HER
TIRED   SLOW FILM   VESUVIUS
THUMB PRINT UPON THUMB PRINT GRINDS THE ASH
OF THIS BLEAKC MOMENT INTO ME
THE DIRTY LIGHT   DINGY IN THE CURTAINS

120. STAY ANOTHER WEEK

I won't know why but lately it seems
the tears are flowing easy, and life
has been so full of uncertainty.
I often think of leaving you,
but I stay another week anyway,
waiting for the puzzle to fall in place.
But the time turns too slow
and my time is so short
and winter is turning into spring.
I want to fly with you,
but I'm afraid we have tickets
to a different plane, I don't know yet,
and you don't either, and
the weeks that pass
might still make our tears
flow down a single cheek.
I also want to fly away from you,
but you've become so much a part of me,
and the truth is just another lie,
so why not take destiny in hand,
and risk the ups and downs another day.
You've brought me back to life it's true,
you've brought me love and affection,
you've shared my laughter and tears,
you took me from a bad track
and put your needle in my veins,
I always come back for more…
When I'm away I can't recall your name
because your face is buried in my heart.
Your voice tells me one thing,
but your arms tell another story.
        It seems the world is moving the way I want
        because I've left the stars alone
    And yet I cry when I can't recall my name.
    And I weep when I see the things I've become
    And I laugh when I hear the songs of misery
    I am hard on myself and hard on you
    because I see the day when a single word
    will seem completely true.
    Oh come all ye good doctors
    say how it's supposed to be
    but I smile when I'm full

and I cry when I'm empty.
In the end maybe
the highway will be my faithful dog
we on a leash to each other
We build each other little bridges, baby,
but I have so much traffic to you
and the river never changes course.
I find it hard to live for just today
because I've been drifting so long
and I want to let down a new sail,
(Don't) take a sunny day to sail away with me
and vanish in the morning,
don't leave me oarless on the open sea.
Sometimes everything seems ok
and sometimes I feel like such a fool
I don't have the strength to say goodbye
I wonder if I have the strength to stay.
You're so concerned about your emptiness
lately it seems that's what you're full of.
    But when I offer to fill your heart
    You tell me you don't care.
    and I feel so stabbed. You talk about love,
    But you don't really care.
    You've been trying hard, You talk
    about beauty, but you're full of fear,
    you're full of sorrow for your sad state,
    your sorrow is your only meaning
    when you cry like that.
You're running from me, baby,
but I also see you running from yourself.
You blame me for the sorrows,
but I also suffer, I didn't make the world,
and what does it matter
if you cry when you're alone,
when we're together that is in the past.
Your strength is fantasy,
fantasy my weakness.
So when you have your visions
you don't even see me
holding you with these tender arms
your eyes are in the future
your eyes are in the distance
you dream dreams of childhood
childhood you think as it was
you dream of the farthest islands
your thoughts run faster

than the far-flying endless telephone lines.
Oh I know I shouldn't talk
I've had even longer to be messed up.
    I have walked through an inferno
    my mind gasping like a fish on sand
    strangers have held my head
    while I puked in my despair.
    But that religion is gone
    I mailed the cross away,
    I tore up the list of sacred words
    I threw out the honor roll of saints,
    and I've been trying so hard
    to make my stand.
    You say I see no beauty,
    you're wrong, only I see through the illusion
    of skin-deep beauty.
    I am the meaning of my words
    I am very careful in my choice.
    though somehow I always seem to turn out wrong.
I told you I love you,
and as your eyes closed gray with meaning,
the wind blew the frozen letters away.
Quicksilver shimmering, touch it and it contracts.
    It's true you've tried to bring love
    but invitations to an empty house bring only regret.
You feel afraid of love returned,
you feel evil in the exchange,
you walk in your cathedral
with the mud of human feelings on your feet.
If I were dreaming, and if I saw in you an angel,
yes, I guess, I could feel wrong,
knowing what I know, feeling as I feel.
But I see you only as a person,
with only the glow of true affection,
and I can only resent it
when you spit your angel shit at me.
But having said these things I am tired again
soon you'll have alittle time for me again
Oh baby how wrongly I accused you
When I thought those things of you,
when I doubted your words,
those times when I hated you.
Now, even though you hurt me,
even though you hurt me,
even while you hold and kiss me,
I love you more than I don't.

I have faith in my survival –
something a falling angel doesn't.
In the end all things will be equal
the good times, the bad, will fall away.
I'm just waiting for the revelations
as they come, I'll try real hard to be good,
I'll really try to remember my medicines,
I'll wait morning after morning
and pray each night to be better.
I've had a dream of being Jesus Christ…

121.   LOVE: IBID

1. And now baby
   I have changed a little, you have made me change,
   I loved you in a way you did not love me,
   I love you the way you loved me,
   You seem to love me as I loved you,
   I don't think I can love you loving me as I loved you.
2. We are doing a heavy trip full of confusions.
   I am confident, I know you are too.
3. What beautiful but scary exchanges are these?
   --Phenomenon we have noticed: how well our bodies fit
   --How well our minds coincide,
   and finally, how we seem to wear each other's attitudes
   The way we trade our shirts and sweaters.
   > And how we antagonize, how we anachronize,
   > each other, how we often are not wearing
   > the same shirt, the same sweater, the same head.
4. We are trying on each other's many facets
   Lost in the attic of our private lives.
   Near the bed of our sexual exultation
   unavoidably—the masks, the shirts
   of the barriers of our limitations of
   our ignorances our fears and superstitious,
   our seesaw desires, though, to cling,
   > yet, to repel, to run,
   > and maybe
   > to run from what we are able to LEARN
   > back to our private theme parks.
5. We are at the mercy of our feelings.
   Children are we, prone to exhaust ourselves,
   cry, laugh, cry again as the rain,
   sun, the wind in the leaves, the hunger,
   thirst, the lice and other comic conspiracies,
   dictate.
6. We aren't, we are, we refuse to be, we would like to be,
   dependent.
7. Oh sister, wife, mother, little girl,
   lover, despiser,
   joy and pain!

122.   CONNECTICUT

It's all here, and I carry you in my soul
Everywhere on earth that I go.
Wind, seasons, stars.

      A humming in the quilted hay lodes.
      The bird, gurgling, softly visits.
      Spring, gently, intrudes.

Trees, leaves, water.

      Connecticut trees, their bark armored
                  gray for winter;
      Melting ice, on sandpaper bark
      in me. ....

123. FUN WHILE, FUTILE

You're in my mind, and my heart, in my structure,
You're in my eyes, in my blood, in my fingers,
lovely dreamer wearing our thoughts.
I've got you boarded up with driftwood
and salvage from a silk mill.
I've got you shining through my window,
I've got you jumping in my river,
You've got me lying on your leaves,
trying on your clothes,
flying on your Peter Pan-Am.
You've got me, I've got you,
we've got places to go,
things to do, before tomorrow
becomes yesterday.
Let me cruise through your eyes
because I'm young and strong,
I'll bring you news of tomorrow before long.
So stay inside my railway
stay with me in the pumpkin coach.
I'll sit beside you forever,
and tell you what I'll never need to say,
and I'll promise you things you'll never
really need, just to fill your suitcase,
my presence—Sunny Fool, Sunny Fool...

124.   SOLAR MILK

Dear heart in my breast,
locus of half my sickness,
my brain the other aching half,
how I infect myself
with this muddled desire!
Such distraction my malady,
such malady my distraction,
toxic distillation scouring the beds
of my blood's river, the musseled
beaches of my thoughts' ocean!

My own disposition
is the poison of my life.
The world is me
I abhor the world, and
thereby abhor myself.

Come, blessed contradiction,
numb the quadrilles of my prison.
Come, come, dear berries of day,
oozing the sweet sun's milk,
rub away the noxious sleep around my eyes!

Aye, this fevered throe
shakes my head in yes's and no's,
makes the giving hand a fist,
the poet's tongue a sour, cringing twist,
and love's death's soliloquy a prolog
                    to the golden hours.

125. BEACH/FOREVER

It has always bothered me
      vaguely
that in this sea of dreams
my dreamship should
choose to run aground
      softly
on the open armed trees...
darkness dancing with light;
bowers of spring blossoms...
blends of grassy green and blue sky...
bosom of turned black earth puddings...
      and
HOUSE cornering on life and death.
(maybe I should run;
for my small FOREVER.)

126. MIRROR TREE/EARTH

- - - Spade my loam and be my shady leaves.
I will be your tree and you my earth.

127.   ZEN

Our lives are mosaics of emotion.
Together, we spin worry and joy.
The implanted anxieties seek survival;
the past, revival; growing up more difficult.

Every day, new. Discovery is unfamiliar.
Not so boxed, we face at every moment
an infinity of choices. Reject all, and
there remains no guide firm in anything.

Freedom is a harried cross.
Self-imposed. And then the anxiety,
trying not to feel self-pity.
Overloaded. No circuit room left for pity.

Reality is a harsh morning light.
Ago, morning light was harsh reality.
In freedom, also, sharp reversals.
The beat remains steady. We?

--Avoid unnecessary concern for self.

128. IMP

Every time you say you love me
I watch your eyes turn distant
Every time you hold me
I feel emptiness between your arms
Baby I'm tired of kissing the heels
of dreams revealed to little girls
I am Jesus and have my dreams to run from
Mickey Mouse has nothing over you.
You are the queen of lonely aces
You never say no, you never say yes
You only smile until they touch you
Then you bite, then you run, howling.
Let's trip to your kingdom
Let's enjoy this tyranny
Your whips are made of glances
Your chains are made of smiles
And all I can do is run away
YesyesI can only leave.

129.   LAUGHING, SHE ATE ME

Darling, This sweet....Treasury...
    For a while   let me be your Aton
    your Orpheus and your Bacchus

    Let us   like leaves
    rustle secrets   rubbing together
      in the dark.
For a while,   let me be your Tristan, your
Cliges, your Romeo, your Cyrano, your Caesar
    Let us   together   live
    as though we always did and ever shall.
    Let me put my   jokes
    in your blue eyes.
    Let me put my   bottle
    to your mouth.
    Let me put my   radio
    into your small hands.
For as long as may be   let me be your
blanket, your pillow, your bed, your own dark room.
    Let down your sunny stream of hair.
    Beg slaughter, smiling,
    let my sword take you, break you, wake you
      where you most want.
Be my wife, my sister, my mother, my daughter, my lover.
These were your words to me: You are my lover, my son,
   and my father...for as long as maybe...
I said to you: I'd like to eat you.
You said to me   I'd like to be eaten.
I'm breathless, the globe stops turning
and she takes my pencil firmly in hand
to start writing love notes while
we sing together in harmony,
wailing union on extra loud radio.

MARGINAL & FOOTNOTES

En Proc
vent. Afr.
ille inven.
magn. vent.
atque flum.
at mult.
ingenia--

Iov.--

    wistful   far-shot missive,
Shubbi-
luliuma,   questing Hat-
           shep-sut: For your daughter,
Anti-
mony from Punt, slaves, lignum Africanum,
E-
gyptian daughters, eyes blacked against the sun,
this great king+I shall offer mine own Son.

                                           Ex cavat
                                           Schlie-
                                           mann
                                             Ilium
                                           HOREMHEB
                                           HATHOR
                                             ISIS

                                           Evans...
                                           Minos...
                                           Crete...

Dawn. Mesopotamian. Ox age.
Sargon. Akkad. Highway.
Waxen seal on letter, on tomb, on doorway,
on chattels, on cattles, on his finger-ring.

Ikhnaton fanciful demigod   fanciful fearful demi-
                   -Glaucomus-   urge,
       ,anachron to th' imaginative world.

Domne, a maid awaits.
Hear, leaf dross, fall stew in our courtyard:
                                      Sinus of
descending darkness.
                                      Porphyry;
                            agate cat's eye. ba. ka.
                            ankh. to the hot gold sand.

131.   CONSENVOYE

The quick-in and quick-out
Modern way. Rained though,
gratuitous, the spirit presented itself
    as of old.
We gave thanks by those blessings.
Wine was brought, turkey was bought,
thought best its steam glaze up
Blaze, cheer through these entrails
themselves of the kneeling wash wives
beating their knotted soakings at the
    river side.

[Rue des Moulins]

132.   BIRD SONG (LAMENT)

Your Oriole flight is
   apprehended --
You fall, banded,
   land, on the rooftops.
     There, tar gums yr feathers--
  Inca, Inca, yr dreams
are memory.
Your journey is ended.
Your wings are crushed.
   What never was.
   never will be.

133.   LOST LOVE, BLUE EYES

Last space ship in, the space age is over.
It was too far to America, and we have
rediscovered god in the unfathomable
sea where we have finally realized the
meaning of ∞.
    Dear Faith, dawn still creeps every aging day
    with pink fingers through the green
    and dew beyond my window - -
    as it always has.
And lost love as surely as dawn
turns into dry summer day.   She
went away. I passed from her mind
like a heavy stone. Adolescent fantasy?
Read on. It's all in the stones, like
the Mountain's face. Critique, like
theology and like ∞, is brushed aside
by pink fingers dripping with dew.
I have rediscovered $\Omega\infty\Omega$. I tear from
a stoned heart this thought: fly far,
my love, my dear sweet friend
    of a past year,
    of a shared dream,
my beloved companion. Fly far,
let many dewy dawns rise out of
your blond hair. May those marvelous
blue eyes of yours often rise from
shadow into sunlight, your pupils
contracting in twin clear blue flashes.
You take with you a piece of my heart,
far as long as you remember me.
And I, you. Faith is my prayer,
love my hawk-borne gift. Far, far,
fly, memory, swift but homeless thought!

134. BARGAIN

Oh if I could have you back
I'd bargain all my ambitions
and conquests against your
soft mind-and-body empathy
beside me in my car.

When I die I think I'll scream
and make a last failing grasp
toward all the selves I could have been.

Yet they, like you, never were –
and if they might have been,
Time, time inexorable
vanishes as unused codes
of past and could alike.

Day is the choice,
dusk the sentence,
night its execution.

I swear to you now,
before these witnesses—
Yearning, Melancholy, deep
Volcanic Grief, and also
a Love shamed by meaningless scribbles
and acts transformed into their own atrophy—
I would give all other futures
If I could only have you back again.

135.   SUM, ESSE, FUI, FUTURUS

when I said good-bye to this girl, now,
somewhere, deep inside me, was a rumbling I know tomorrow or
sometime soon will erupt in me - - no Krakatoa, but reiteration…

for dreams, the Indian Summer wind pushes around the corners
under the dark moonlit gables where leaves drive shadows once only, each,
over concrete pores.

the up, the down of the dry branches,
is the echo of my welled tears.
oh, another, mother, again,
and I am mute to bring back with spells
the yesterdays enchantment shrove.

my poor mind, little ship, against all nothingness,
when I am alone, the spectres gain flesh and well up in words,
like images from a tarny well.mother, father, best friend, love less however,
for there and there only can we say good-bye, hello, good-bye, only in
love, most talked-about and supernal of all the emotions…

the past, farther than distance, gone, never was,
I too, and cry for all the was and all the won't be.

136.   SENSES, SENSELESS

do you smell the roses, the moss, the grass and bath steam?
the evening, the sunlight, the trees growing in the windows?
the faint cigarette smoke, the blue haze of gasoline?
do you feel the urge to write,
the passion fro a close and silent friend?
do you thrive on time and time alone,
and do you offer hot green summery solitude?
a meadow? a flight of bees, a flutter of wings?
have you a table whose napkins are windscattered,
a glass tinkling with ice and fountains of pinprick soda?
careless legs on a chipped white chair, sandals,
muscles and soft skin, roundness of pliant
flesh trim and ever-undulant with quick unpretending motions?
have you a free day, a cigarette, a light, a night to spare,
a little time to delay your promises to yourself?

137.   HAIKU (FAN)

Oh, this heat! –Fan: ON
--your petals like spring water,
cool air to inhale!

138.   CHILD: COLOPHON

Come, child, sit by the stove.
Outside the storm may howl,
The rain be cold and sleek
Over the backs of the trees,
But you shall read, read,
and be lost into a brighter world.

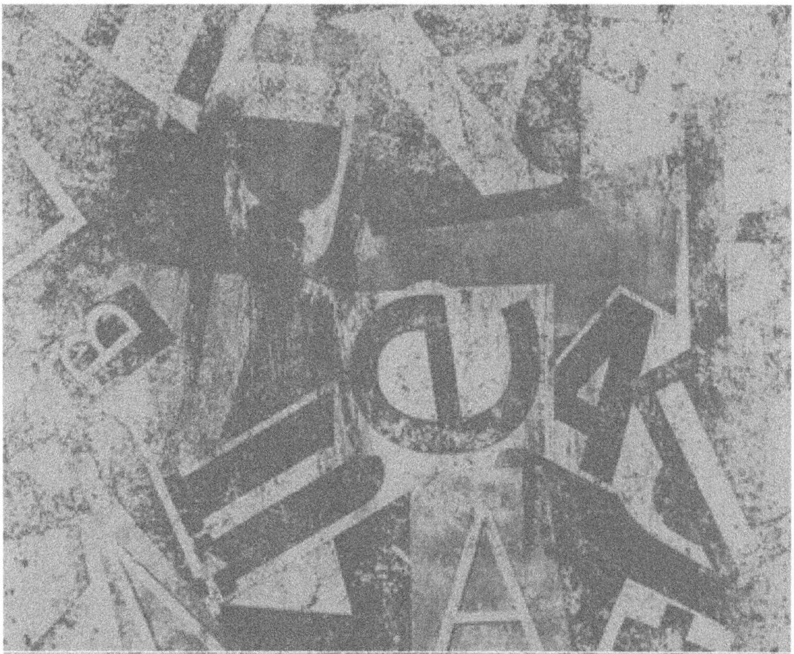

15¶
20¶
16¶
17¶
19¶
22¶
18¶
21¶
23¶